The Helper's Crossroads

Shaun McBride

Dear Emily,
This is a special copy for you, my love! I hope you enjoy your journey into my brain!
With lots of love ♡
Shaun

The Helper's Crossroads
Shaun McBride
2021
Published independently

Please Read:

This book is a pay-as-you-feel and contribute-as-you-can production, except a minimum is imposed to cover printing costs. If you cannot pay for the book but would like to contribute a gift you have instead, please get in contact through the website. If you don't feel comfortable doing this, I only ask that you go weave some connections in your area.

Beyond this, I invite you to please share this book with others, in part or in whole, but do not sell it, except with my permission. If you do share only in part, please include as much as you can to avoid being taken out of context.

If you have received this book from someone else, or have bought the paperback from Amazon, please consider leaving a donation or contributing in some way at helperscrossroads.com

I reserve the right to change the usage rights of this book at any time if the need arises.

Acknowledgements

My parents, for giving everything for us.
Daniel Isaac, Calum Awcock & the rest of the Gaskell Garden Project, for showing me true community, for starting me on this path and continuing to walk alongside me.
Stephen Agnew, for our decade-long, endless discussions on philosophy that have been crucial to the development of the thoughts that underpin this book.
Aidan Baron, Scott Diamond and Dan Klapaukh, for providing me with endless support as we figured out together the practical application of our values in the professional world, which is now summed up in this book.
Cormac Russell and the Nurture Development team, for always seeing & finding ways to use people's gifts, for taking a chance on me, and for creating the conditions in which this book could be written.
Melissa Garside, whose remarkable gifts have yet to find the recognition they certainly deserve, and whose influence runs so deep through every page that the book couldn't have been written without it.

Contents

Foreword	5
Introduction	10
Part 1 The Helper's Crossroads	
Chapter 1: My Story	19
Chapter 2: The Origins & Development of the Helper's Crossroads	31
Chapter 3: The Helper's Crossroads	35
Chapter 4: The "To/For" Road	45
Chapter 5: The "Through" Road	95
Chapter 6: The "By" Road	122
Chapter 7: The "With" Road	139

Part 2: Springboards for Discussion

Chapter 8:
The Roles We Play — 157

Chapter 9:
Community Permaculture: Principles of Sustainable Organisation Design — 163

Chapter 10:
What do communities create? — 195

Chapter 11:
Health & Healthism — 203

Chapter 12:
Social Prescribing — 217

Chapter 13:
Online Bumping Spaces — 225

Conclusion — 231

Foreword

By Cormac Russell

Wayfinders have always been essential to human adaptiveness. Each time we commune with our surroundings, we must necessarily find ways to be more human together; more natural with nature, and more receptive to the shifting sands and vibrant waves of our tribal wanderings, and our planetary and universal evolution.

As we wander out from our homeplaces or plot our homecomings from far flung shores, we require a compass of sorts to gain our bearings. Down through the ages, peoples have found their collective way to adopt to their environments through such compasses.

Though it ought to be noted that the lion's share of our ancestors were not cartographers, they were eco-explorers; nomads; foragers and survivors. Our forebearers, for the most part, were searching, not planning. They embodied the epigram: the map is not the territory. And so they made their way in deep communion and struggle with the territories they moved through and which moved through them. The wayfinding tradition I am recalling is evident in the cuisines, dialects, and cosmologies of their cooperative adventures, in the ways their children were raised, how art was spate forth and curated, how customs were practiced and stories shared. In short, their particular ways of adapting to given local places, down through human history, became manifest in what we today call culture. Some of these cultures still exist at least in memory, but sadly most are lost to us, and we are the poorer for it.

In many ancient traditions, talismans and amulets, believed to be holders of magical powers, were used to protect, heal, and guide, and to ward off any external force that would harm their cultural life.

This book is both a compass and a talisman. It extends a deep bow to our ancestors and more recent wisdom traditions in the fields of community development, philosophy, social justice and ecology, to mention but a few. It owes much to many wisdom traditions, and so, you will encounter Gandhian overtones, the principles of permaculture and Marxian dialectic, fluently and accessibly tapped and sometimes reimagined. Yet, this is not a mashup of various interesting theories, rather these theories are used by the author, as multiple lenses through which to look afresh at modern life and search out a preferred future. Just as the Book of the Marvels of the World, more popularly known as The Travels of Marco Polo, is not about the instruments Polo used to chart his course, it is rather a travelogue written down by Rustichello da Pisa from stories shared with him by the explorer while they were both in prison together, about his adventure through Asia, and the magical experiences he had at the court of Kublai Khan. Likewise, this book, is about Shaun McBride's adventures with life and its deep ecology.

The book, The Helper's Crossroads, like all good compasses and talismans, is fundamentally grounded in reverence for and reference to places and indigenous ways. It does not suffer from the affliction of moral relativism, but nor does it preach a closed doctrine. At the core of this book, Shaun has used a framework which I first developed a decade ago and which is described in detail in my book Rekindling Democracy-A Professional's Guide to Working in Citizen Space. I called this navigation framework "The Helper's Crossroads". My intention was that it would be freely used by authentic helpers with expansive moral imaginations to curb colonial impulses, which have so profoundly harmed communities, down through history. This is exactly what has happened here in the pages to follow, as with Marco Polo's use of navigation frameworks available to him at his time of setting sail from his homeplace, Shaun, using my original framework, while respecting its core insight, has innovated around it's edges, to explore questions that matter to him, such as the rising and worrying phenomenon of "healthism".

He also invites us as readers, to seek out new adventures in our own helping journeys, by considering our territory and way ahead with reference to his next generation version of the Helper's Crossroads. In doing so, he helps us see different places and applications for the framework. By tilting the lens, in new directions and placing accents and inflections in the grammar of the Helper's Crossroads, he calls our attention towards some fresh dilemma's in navigating a post-colonial future.

Shaun's book excites me because it clearly reveals an imperial sleight of hand on the part of institutionalists, that is not always revealed or made apparent *vis-a-vis* my original framework. His next generation version exposes the clear and present danger that institutions can, on the face of it, speak of community development and working in an asset-based community development way, but solely so that they can better extract community assets for their institutional objectives. Like the Pharaohs and Priestly classes of old, who believed their versions of salvation warranted the harvesting of local assets, Shaun helps us to see how modern institutions can also work "through" communities to achieve their so-called "worthy" ends, be that "health", "safety", or "progress" more generally. Just as Pharaohs used the assets of communities to build their fantasy gateways towards the immortality of the Gods, so too can modern professionals backed-up by their institutions.

Shaun, is a modern Wayfinder and social explorer; his book will help others as they deepen their own wayfinder instincts and resistance to the Pharaoh's call, and will help insulate all those who read it from the excesses of empire that lurk behind the veil of good intentions.

Cormac Russell, Dublin, 2021

Introduction

The world is full of people who want to help others. Exactly who people should or are willing to help has varied and been debated throughout history, but that we are in some way genetically or socially encoded to help at least *some* others is pretty well identified. But what people throughout history have identified is that helping is not actually that straightforward. Just like those who jump in rivers to save another but only create two casualties instead of one, in lots of ways, we can end up increasing the total suffering in the world, even if that's only from our own suffering.

This book is for helpers who want to be more conscious about the way they help and the effects it has on those they help. By proposing and illustrating a framework called "The Helper's Crossroads", I hope to be useful to others in deciding how to help people in the best way.

When we go out intending to help, whether we know it or not, we find ourselves standing in the middle of the Helper's Crossroads. And many of us are standing there, gazing out at the many roads that lie before us, wondering which one will work best. You see many fellow helpers huddled around an old wooden signpost which informs travellers of the names of each road. You'll become more familiar with these terms, and will find more explanations, later on. For now, they are:

- Doing something **To** or **For** others - these are actually two parallel roads that basically form a single highway. On one side lies exploitation, and on the other, charity & paternalism.
- Doing something **Through** others - Along this road, one finds where you achieve *your* goals through the actions of others, also known as community engagement and traditional volunteering
- Doing something **With** others - This road looks like shared decision making or co-production, where you are invited to support others to achieve their goals with your resources
- Something being done **By** people themselves - This is the road on which sits Asset-Based Community Development, intuitive eating and any other person-led or citizen-led change. It is change decided by and done by the very people it affects.

We can imagine it all started when, one person, not wanting to appear as confused as the rest of us, boldly strolled past us, and confidently walked down the road the signpost reliably calls "**To/For**". One person followed. Then two. Then three.

Before long, the road to "To/For" had all the hallmarks of a well-trodden path. A steady stream of people down this road now entices all those who stop at the signpost to follow the crowd. Over time, this road has developed many fancy additions. The road on either side is lined with lavish buildings for the traveller. The path becomes known as the righteous path, and many people who carry respect, like philosophers, professors and politicians cry loudly about its virtue. Educators stand at the crossroads, providing lots of information about this road (for a fee). Comparatively, the other roads seem to be complete unknowns. People come to be aware of lots of stories of those who have taken this path and have done very well for themselves; they've found a stable financial arrangement and you could too.

Not everyone who set off down this road is convinced this was the right way, however. Along the way down this road, we see that some of the people on this road are now driving fancy cars, while those they help are still struggling. We see exploitation and corruption. We also see that some of the people we'd like to help aren't as well treated as we'd like. We see that in many ways, we are keeping those people "needy" so we can carry on being "good people" or philanthropists.

Some hesitantly carry on down this path, some a bit further than others, and some never stop. This is a legitimate and valid course of action. Ahead lies security, behind lies insecurity, and especially in insecure times like ours, with mortgages & families to ensure, nobody can be blamed for walking towards security and doing anything they can to bury any hesitant thoughts.

Some of us, however, turn back and return to the crossroads. In recent days, enough people are turning back that the road to "Through" and "With" have started to look like major roads too. But, amongst the great hustle & bustle of the Helper's Crossroads is hidden the entrance to a little dirt track, which our trusty signpost calls "By". A few helpers, for whatever reason, have chosen this path.

I am one of those who turned back and ended up travelling this road, and I'm very lucky to have come alongside a great many travellers on this road who have helped me navigate its twists & turns, who have provided a tent where there are no rest stops and a humorous story or two to pass the time. Fellow travellers have taken the time to teach me their craft along this road. Some have called it, "permaculture", some "intuitive eating" and others "asset-based community development (ABCD)". This book is predominantly written from the perspective of ABCD but is informed by, and allied with other perspectives that share its values.

When chancing upon the Helper's Crossroads, it's natural to be so absorbed by the bright lights of the To/For road that you don't even see the other roads. I felt if I had been given a map of the crossroads, that told me where each road leads, what sights you might see along the way, what are the pros and cons of each road, then I might have been able to choose a better road the first time around.

This book is my attempt at a map. I am still a young traveller on these roads, but in my time, I've listened intently to the stories of experienced travellers along each of the roads. I hope to compile these stories into something that makes sense for travellers like me turning up to the crossroads and wondering which path to take.

The road names may not make much sense to you yet, but they will soon. Suffice here to say, however, that I am a lover of the "By" road, but there are caveats. This, as far as it is possible to put my own biases to one side, is a map that will detail the terrain to be found on each road without judgement, but there will definitely still be bias. As someone interested in creating health in the community, the road I find most suitable is the "By" road. I hope if I ever need surgery, however, that my surgeons have taken the "To/For" road. There is no "better" road, only different ones for different purposes. I hope to give an impartial account of the roads to help you navigate to the right one.

Furthermore, there is no obligation to take any road. Those who choose to take a road are in no way morally superior or better people to those who choose not to or cannot. "No road" is as good as any other road. A chapter later in the book will explore in greater detail the principal danger of the Helper's Crossroads - namely, a moral pressure to be helpful and the determination of self- and social-worth based on how helpful you are.

Let's get a few things out of the way before we go any further, however:

This book is wrong. There will be lots of mistakes and misunderstandings that will become clearer over the course of time. I say this to say that <u>all models</u> and the books that propose them are wrong, but some are still useful. I'm not aiming to be 100% correct, but to be different and useful. I'm not preaching the one truest truth at you from a pedestal of expertise, but relating the experiences of myself and others. If you find the models I discuss here useful maps to your world too, then that's great. If not, please share with the world so that we can all develop more useful models.

In this vein, this is not a scientific essay drawing on external evidence to try to convince you to hold the same opinion and model as me. You will deliberately find almost no reference to studies or external evidence. Throughout, I trust that I'm discussing experiences we all share, and that you will find in your own life experiences that relate to the principle of what I'm saying. Therefore, I'm not teaching you anything new, I'm only pointing out things that were already there that you might have not attached meaning or significance to - just like a random group of stars you've always gazed at can suddenly become the shape of a spoon just by it being pointed out. The stars haven't changed, and you weren't taught any new skill, just began to see the same things differently. I am hoping to show you a language that you can use to describe concepts that have always existed in your mind, but struggled to articulate.

In being upfront about the fallibility of my work, I'm hoping to disrupt in a small way the traditional publishing paradigm: that you have to be an educated expert, that there is no room for mistakes. By not having the attributes of many authors - I am not a professor or widely educated and published in my field - I hope to show that you don't need to be to share. By self-publishing, I'm trying to disrupt the idea that only people who are chosen by publishing companies can share. By not paying for a proofreader or editor, and by only using Google Documents to write and my community to check, I'm trying to show that finances should also not be a huge barrier. I want to see more publications that are more diverse from citizens relating their diverse experiences, not more publications from experts. I hope how I've created this work helps create that world.

Finally, a note on language. I'm painfully aware that what I'm trying to do here is "trying to fight colonialism in a colonised tongue"[1]. That is, in an attempt to lift up the community space, I'm using words that are unavoidably tainted by their use *outside* the community space, by institutions and others who use those words to further their own agenda, for manipulation, for restriction, and not for liberation. A particularly problematic word in this book is "model", a word that is often used not to describe just a point of view, as equally valid as others, or a lightly-held framework, but a concept that demands fealty, a competitive force, and a tool used by institutions to further their agenda. As we will see in the chapter on the "Through" road, we'll also see how the word "community" itself could be added to an "At Risk" category. This poses an ethical paradox for me as a writer, whether to pursue "clean" words free of this association, or to use my writing to reclaim those same words. For the purposes of this book, I will do the latter, using this caveat to make this process conscious and intentional. This does not undo the damage that using the wrong words can do, and I'm very open to hearing feedback and altering vocabulary in a future edition, but making this clear is the least-harmful approach I believe I can take.

---

[1] A line from Lowkey & Akala's "Behind My Painted Smile", a UK hip-hop track.

Part 1

The Helper's Crossroads

Chapter 1: My Story

Why tell my story?

I'll begin the book with an account of my personal travels. There are a few reasons for doing this, however, please feel free to skip this story as it's not necessary to know.

Firstly, I do not tell my story to put myself on a pedestal. On the contrary, I'm telling my story so that readers can firmly take me off any pedestal they might assume me to be on by being the author of this book. Also, it's very easy if you're unsure about the road you've taken for your negative self-talk to jump on this and use it against you. The critical part of your mind might tell you that if you were better, you wouldn't have been fooled by the glamour of the "To/For" road to start with and taken a different road like those you see on the "By" road. I know because I've been there too.

But what you often don't see is that almost all of us who now advocate for the "By" road have travelled the same path. I am no different. I came the very long way round too. With a military father, youthful years spent in the Cub Scouts and Air Cadets, followed by 3 years as a Royal Naval Officer, leaving only to join the ambulance service and train as a paramedic, I started out as the textbook definition of an institutionalised helper.

The world seemed at this time like it was reducible to some simple truths: people don't know what's good for them, and even if they did, the good they could attempt to make would be inferior to that made by the specialist knowledge and tools at the disposal of institutions & professionals. So, of course, I came to the conclusion that all human progress could only be made through improving institutions. I hope through relating my story, I can show you how I came from these beliefs to the ones espoused in this book.

The second reason is that I also am very aware of my privilege, biases and the way my specific experiences change the way I look at the world. For example, while I wouldn't consider myself an anarchist, I have been influenced strongly by anarchists I've met along the way who do a huge amount of grassroots community organising. Particularly, they have shown me just how much can be achieved outside of any organised formal structures by a loose, horizontal group. The result of this is that I am probably more averse to organisation structure and bureaucracy than maybe it deserves. Writing as a white, western, cis-gender, heterosexual male also brings with it a whole host of paradigm-influencing lenses that I'll probably never be fully aware of. So, the second reason for telling my story is that others may be able to improve on my model by using my story to backwards-engineer and subtract out my biases.

My Story

So, having set off down the To/For road in earnest, what happened for me to turn back and explore other roads and, eventually, kicking and screaming the whole way, come round 180 degrees to now spend my time as a champion for citizen's expertise in defining the important goals for their community and the benefits of allowing them to solve it?

There were three areas in which my transformation took place. The first is my experience of finding a positive, accepting, loving community for the first time in my life in the Gaskell Garden Project in Manchester, and the way that others, particularly those who carried labels like "refugee" or "mentally ill", also found personal transformation in the same space. The second is my experience of the limits of institutional work and the direct experience of health inequities through my work as a paramedic. The third, the last straw, took place over four months on the Greek island of Lesbos, working in the small clinic for the largest refugee camp in Europe, Moria, seeing the harm NGOs inflict in "disaster aid environments".

The Gaskell Garden Project

A chance meeting with Dan Isaac, the de facto 'head' and founder of the Gaskell Garden Project (GGP), while fixing my punctured bike tyres, led me to begin my transformation. I had recently left the Navy, moving to Manchester, where I knew just one other person in the city. The GGP allowed me to find community and, energised to do some 'good' in the world, the GGP allowed me to discover my assets & use them.

While I, as a white, straight, cis-gendered, well-spoken, straight-A student from a secure household, had been privileged enough to have never been labelled out of community life, the general decay in community life around me had left me without ever having truly experienced a real community, except for some faint memories of community life in rural Cornwall when I was very young (the late 90s). My search for this community is what attracted me to the camaraderie of the military and probably also the close-knit family of the ambulance service – neither of which, for various reasons, were premised on true inclusion.

The Gaskell Garden Project changed this. The GGP was rooted in permaculture and centred on an allotment where we grew food. Anyone was invited to grow with us and, as Dan worked in a refugee & asylum seeker-led legal organisation (RAPAR) where the groundwork of eschewing labels and paternalism had been long established, I grew food alongside many people traditionally labelled and fixed, whether students defined as "lonely" or refugees & asylum seekers defined as "vulnerable". Over time, we began to cook & eat the food together at "Pay As You Feel Meals".

In this association, I found a loving community where I could be the authentic me, an environment where I could undergo personal transformation. I also watched as those who would traditionally be excluded from the cooking experience ("don't worry, just sit there and let us do the work") or who would only be allowed to grow food in a carefully controlled, funded environment where they are expected to declare their problems & allow themselves to be "fixed" by others, could instead just show up, be themselves and contribute their gifts if they wanted to.

At first, I thought we were doing something unique – we once gave a presentation on what we called "social permaculture" – but later in the story, I learned we were just doing what any true community association does, and what the ABCD (asset-based community development) community has been lifting up for a long time. That doesn't mean I instantly converted to the ABCD way. Seeing the amazing changes around me, but not understanding truly where it was coming from, I was the chief promoter of a move towards scaling up and institutionalisation. I too succumbed to the idea that a good organisation aspires to look like institutions and big charities: policies, funding, employment, measurement, research, rigid decision making structures, minimising risk and constitutions (I told you I was a slow learner). Eventually, I came to understand that the reason I and others found the space transformative was because of the very absence of those things.

At the Gaskell Garden Project, in summary, I experienced first-hand the power of citizens to define the problem and to use their resources to solve it. I experienced the power of spaces where people can contribute, not be fixed. I also experienced the transformative power of being in a community for the first time.

The Ambulance Service and the limits of the institutional world

At the same time as I was experiencing citizen-led change at the Gaskell Garden Project, I experienced the limits of professional-led change within the NHS. Not many people realise, even among those who work inside it, but the ambulance service is very exposed to what professionals call "social deprivation". You constantly find yourself in the same ("poor") neighbourhoods. Not only do traditional "emergencies" (for example, heart attacks or strokes) occur more often there as a result of the very real toll that the stress of economically oppression takes on your body, but also what could be termed a "social emergency" where 999 is the only person someone has to turn to. For example, where someone has a simple, non-injury inflicting trip but has no one to just help them get back up off the floor, or where someone has received such stigmatising care in more "appropriate" settings that they feel that 999 is the only place they can be sure to get help for their problem.

As a result of these experiences, I was led into the realm of the institutional health world called "inclusion health", a subsection of Public Health/Health Promotion which "combats health inequities", which is largely led by a progressive layer of health professionals with a special interest in making sure the service we provide is equitable & inclusive.

My experiences attempting to provide equitable care to my patients in my frontline role, as well as trying to improve services more generally, gave me an appreciation for the limits of the institutional world and how I could 'help' as a helper. However, these limits were not solely from those who you might expect – those in control of tight budgets or those who hold a more conservative mindset – but also from my very well-meaning colleagues, some of whom were unable to step outside of the paternalistic paradigm and create change in the way I was seeing happen at the Gaskell Garden Project, which began most fundamentally with the recognition of the essential competence & capacity of all.

The assumption unquestioned by many in Public Health/Health Promotion/Inclusion Health is that institutions, namely here the Health & Social Care Complex, is at least the primary if not the only producer of health. Out of this assumption arises paternalism – if we are the only producers of health, and if health is inequitable, it must be us who is producing it inequitably, and thus the solution to inequitable health can only be found in institutional reform. In trying to combat the destructive "individual responsibility" or neoliberal model of health, little room is left for understanding how communities & citizens can also create health, which I believe are the most powerful health creators in the equation.

In summary, when it comes to managing disease, it is essential that the Health & Social Care Complex provides an equitable service. However, when it comes to the whole picture of health creation, the Complex forms only a part, but it is here that it can unintentionally overreach into citizen space and actually displace communities & citizens own, more effective, health creation efforts.

The Refugee "Aid" Context

The stage was set in my mind. The jigsaw puzzle was poised to be solved. I had experienced citizen-led change and was convinced its principles were the way forward but had not yet quite completely understood how the institutions I worked in and saw all around me fit into this, but I was beginning to suspect that they couldn't do what citizens could do, and had not yet discovered ABCD as a field. What I needed was a jolt, and I got it when I volunteered in Lesbos, Greece, where I came to really understand the harms of institutional overreach.

While providing medical cover for refugee boat beach landings, I met people as they arrived on the beach, having survived not just the incredibly difficult conditions in their own country but also the traumatic & dangerous journey spanning thousands of miles, of which the sea route to Lesbos was but the perilous finale.

The changes I witnessed in these same people as they attended the clinic over the following months, however, was a rapid transition from a hardy survivor who had all the assets to navigate extreme circumstances to someone who was now assumed to have no assets and was alive only thanks to the grace of Western NGOs and their mostly white, middle-class volunteers. This was not the result of an evil, refugee-demonising agenda aimed at breaking refugees, but of the well-intentioned but essentially imperialist & colonial aid sector.

I saw NGO managers drive around the town in the fanciest sports cars, while the local Greeks could only afford clapped-out vehicles, and the refugees walked for 2 hours in the searing heat from the camp. I saw the 'voluntourists' who had paid thousands of dollars to an NGO and were interested in being around refugees for only as long as it took to get a selfie and tick a box on their CV, but ran in the opposite direction when their perfect beach day was threatened by refugees coming to enjoy the same beach. I saw the long, dehumanising food queues and the abuses of power where favourable treatment was given by the Evangelical organisation who administered food, shelter & clothing to those who officially converted to Christianity. But worst of all, I saw refugees come to internalise the falsehood that kept this state of affairs alive – that they depended on us to survive.

I realised that this wasn't unique to the aid context. It might have been more intense and rapid there, but my friends seeking asylum that I grew food alongside in Manchester had experienced the same process in a slower, more subtle, way, and so had the 'marginalised' people I had tried to help in my job as a paramedic, and in a weird way, so had I, as a citizen, through my whole life. Even though I had ended up on the 'helper' side of the divide, I had swallowed the myth there was nothing I could do about my life or for my community except consume services.

The final straw was being invited to present research at a conference on "Homeless & Inclusion Health" which was held at an extremely fancy hotel in London and charging an entrance fee that I, as a well-paid professional, couldn't afford, let alone someone who is also denied a home or is marginalised. It makes you wonder who are the real beneficiaries of an event like this. It felt no different from the extravagances I saw in Greece and became an obvious example that this is far from being isolated to disaster zones and is in fact totally normal and acceptable in western society.

In that way, the final piece of the puzzle fell into place. The citizen-led change of the Gaskell Garden Project, the inability of the ambulance service and other institutions to do the same thing, and the very real harm that institutional overreach causes, not only in the "aid" context but "at home" too. So when I began to reflect and research all this for a university module on "Humanitarian Assistance" and found out that there were other people who thought the same way, and it was called Asset Based Community Development, I was overjoyed. I felt like I had found 'my people' and something I wanted to dedicate myself to. I decided right then that ABCD was what I wanted to do for the rest of my life. I was so excited that I cold-messaged Cormac Russell on Twitter, who was then and has continued to be, the most welcoming friend and inspirational mentor. I'm incredibly fortunate to have now found myself as an intern assisting Cormac to build the Community Renewal Centre.

And that's the story of how an institutionalised helper got here! I hope my story demonstrates that no one is special, only very few people 'get' ABCD straight away, and we are all on a journey together towards a better future.

Chapter 2:
The Origins & Development of the Helper's Crossroads

First of all, I must acknowledge the intellectual ancestry of my particular interpretation of the "Helper's Crossroads".

You can see below (Fig. 1) the Helper's Crossroads as shared by Cormac Russell & Nurture Development. This is a favourite metaphor of Cormac's and is a critical feature of his account of how communities & institutions interact. Without his intellectual contribution to create this first version of the map, any subsequent version, and this entire book, wouldn't exist.

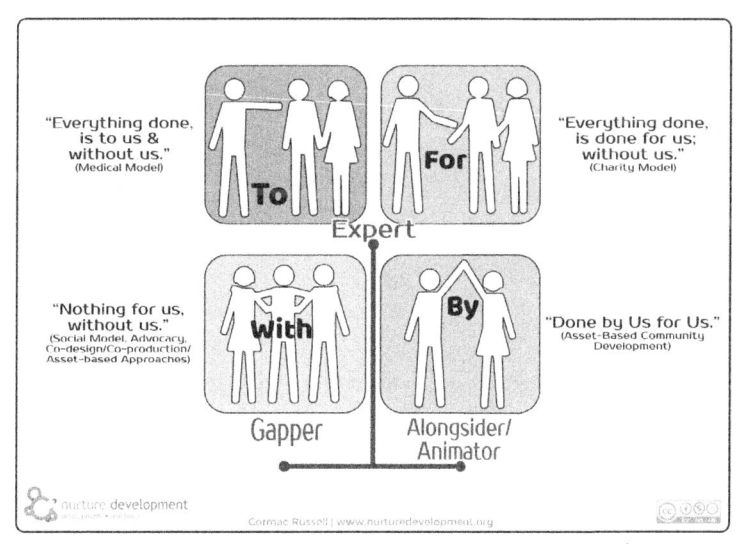

(Fig. 1) - The Original Helper's Crossroads - Cormac Russell & Nurture Development

Secondly, the assumption in our world is that two similar models must be in competition, and that by presenting my own interpretation of the model, that I must be presenting it as more true. I am making this invisible assumption visible so that I can discount it. A small philosophical tangent follows to back up this point, but skip it if you like.

In summary, all models are wrong, some are useful.

What is a model?

We all use models every single day, yet are rarely conscious of them. A model is any mental tool or mental construct that allows us to interact with the world around us. Just like physical tools, they are not passive. The condition of all life is that we must interact with the world outside of our body to meet the energy needs of our cell(s). This would be impossible if the world was pure unpredictable chaos, so we need to make sense of what order there is in the world to meet these needs reliably and to do this, we need to construct models that allow us to interact in a predictable way. These models are as simple as the surface of the earth being solid to political views to the leading edge of physics.

Here, our model, and indeed the model of ABCD in general, is attempting to provide us with some predictable outcomes for the different ways we can help each other.

What is the relationship between a model and truth?

Just as for a map, there is the real territory, the ground we see and feel under our feet, for models there is the objective truth, the real-life experiences of people. Both maps & models are not a perfect representation of their respective real territory. This is recognised in conventional wisdom by the saying "the map is not the territory". Some maps emphasise the layout of roads for the purpose of road navigation (Road Atlas) but ignore undulation, others truthfully reflect the gradients of hills & valleys while not being particularly accurate for roads, others are rough sketches of a garden on the back of a fag packet. All of these maps are wrong in some way, but they have some use.

Similarly, no model is absolutely true. All models - that is, any mental tool that humans use to try to understand the world, exists because it is useful in some way to someone. In fact, it is not proximity to truth that drives models to succeed, but its usefulness to the organism, though more truthful models do *tend* to be more useful. Cormac Russell regularly acknowledges this with his statement that "all models are wrong, some are useful".

Neither the model I propose here, nor Cormac's model from which I have adapted, is true, just a faithful attempt to model truth. Whether you find yourself using my map, or Cormac's, is not down to one being wrong and the other right, or truthfulness, but which one is more useful to you, which one resonates most with you, which one models your reality better.

Viewed through this paradigm, we can dismiss the idea that these two models are in any manner competing. They can co-exist and will serve varying degrees of usefulness to different people with different experiences. Truth is to be found in diversity, and it is in this spirit that I share with you my adaptation of the map, which I found useful when navigating the institutional and community worlds, in the hope that others might find it useful, and that it might spurn more useful offshoots.

Chapter 3:
The Helper's Crossroads

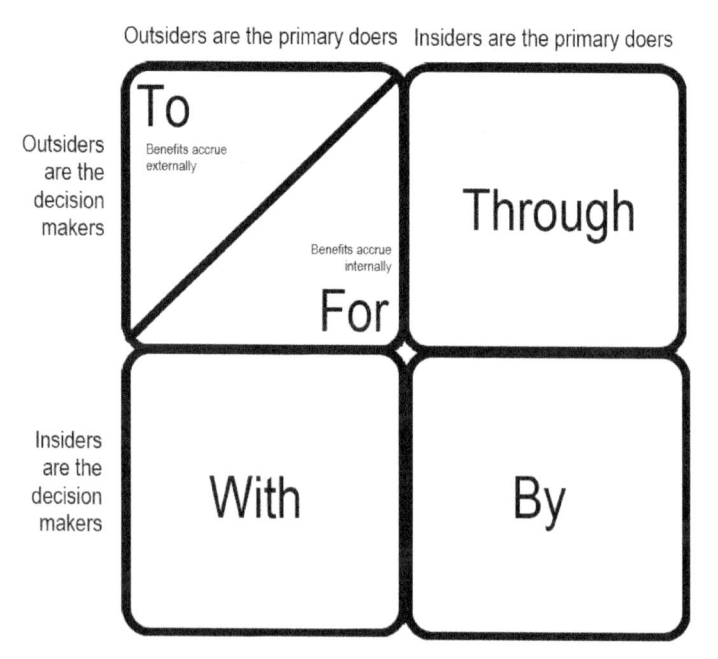

	Outsiders are the primary doers	Insiders are the primary doers
Outsiders are the decision makers	**To** — Benefits accrue externally / **For** — Benefits accrue internally	**Through**
Insiders are the decision makers	**With**	**By**

(Fig 2.) - McBride's Helper's Crossroads

Here I present the map that I use when thinking about change defined & enacted by different actors. Models are not a passive, pointless exercise, but all models are intended to be used actively. Maps are not primarily interesting things to look at, but a way of predicting, if you set off from A, what the journey will look like between A and B, and how you might navigate using those predictions. This model is similar, we intend to use it to predict what the likely outcomes are when change occurs of one sort or another. For example, you may be familiar from ABCD thought on the subject so far that we predict that change that occurs in the "To/For" roads engender dependency and are often met with resistance, while "By" road gives people confidence and develops local capacities.

The Questions

Throughout my ABCD journey, I have seen two recurring questions present themselves as central to figuring out what the likely effect will be of any change:

1. Who is defining what a good life looks like, the question/answer, the change or the problem to be solved? Who are the decision makers?
2. Whose resources will primarily be used to do something about it? Who are the primary doers?

In my view, ABCD is summed up by the answer to these two questions: it is the community that defines the change and are the ones to create it. I noticed that this mapped well onto Cormac's metaphor of the Helper's Crossroads, which was the driving force behind my own interpretation.

Focus on what's strong, not what's wrong

Almost everyone associated with ABCD in some way will be familiar with a different way of summing up ABCD: "Focus on what's strong, not what's wrong" is another of Cormac Russell's favourite phrases. So how does my definition of ABCD relate to this one with which you may be more familiar?

I think the recommendation to not focus on what's wrong is a direction to not go into communities as an "outsider" (in this case, a professional) trying to find a problem. By going into a system trying to diagnose problems that are by definition pre-defined, e.g. loneliness or dementia, the problem is therefore defined by the outsider. Conversely, by not focusing on what's wrong, you create the space for the community to define the problem to be solved or the change they wish to see instead.

Meanwhile, in the second half, I think the prescription to focus on what's strong, is about seeing that there are more assets than the institutional, that the community has its own assets too, and thus allowing those assets to be used to create change.

This phrase is itself a model, and an extremely useful one. It is a simple, one-line, concept that gives us a rule of thumb for helping. Its excellence in achieving this purpose is seen by how fast this 'meme' has spread. However, it is a model, and all models leave out something to emphasise others. Here, the weakness is that its brevity means that sometimes it can be interpreted in different ways.

For this reason, some might have recoiled earlier at my use of the words "defining the problem". The directive to not focus on "what's wrong" can be interpreted as a directive to never talk about anything negative - to not look at communities as having any problems, or to look at needs. This is not my interpretation, though that doesn't necessarily mean that I am right.

For me, ABCD is about absolute freedom & subsidiarity. So, firstly, this means citizens & their communities get to define their situation in any way that they wish. In my view, it is an outside imposition in itself to tell citizens & communities that <u>they</u> cannot define their situation in the negative, as having problems, just as much as it is an outside imposition to tell citizens & communities that they <u>must</u> diagnose problems in their communities or for a professional to do that diagnosing on their behalf.

Secondly, many communities are blighted by very real problems they wish to solve, climate change being a huge one common to us all, as well as institutional racism and economic oppression. To tell citizens & communities that they shouldn't talk about their problems as problems does nothing but alienate.

Lastly, the issue is often purely linguistic. We can often phrase things in both the "positive" and the "negative". For example, if some neighbours come together to pick up litter in their street, as that's an issue they care about, it's not any less ABCD because they define that as "solving the litter problem" instead of "keeping streets clean".

As previously mentioned, my interpretation is that the "Don't focus on what's wrong" is about outsiders/professionals/institutions holding off from defining the situation in their institutional, "needs assessment" way, and instead allow space for the community to define the situation. To limit any community or citizen's capacity to define their situation how they wish - even if that's limiting to the positive - automatically invokes the To/For road.

Insider vs. Outsider

The terms "Insider" & "Outsider" and "Internal" & "External" are likely to be confusing without explanation - and are certainly a drawback of my map - but I believe that the vagueness is necessary in order that the use of the model is applicable to different scales.

My world view is to see everything as networks of components that function to serve a particular purpose, therefore being a "system". This is true of our network of cells (and even organelles) which cooperate to produce complex life, which clearly must confer some sort of reproductive advantage, as well as our networks of citizens that come together to form the human tribe, which similarly confers some reproductive advantage.

If we are to see the world as networks, we must have some way of defining the boundaries of systems. One way we can do this is by defining those who are predominantly affected by any change to a system, and that's the definition I use here. A change to a community in Australia may, over time and through lots of intermediate effects, affect me in the UK in the future, but I am not the predominantly affected party by this change and can therefore be defined as "outside" the system to some degree. Meanwhile, the members of that same community will be directly affected by the change, and therefore can be defined as "inside" the system. Despite the huge complexity of our systems, I think that we can intuitively, and with a sufficient degree of accuracy and precision, distinguish roughly where the boundary sits pretty quickly if we accept that it's the boundary is not one we have to tightly define and be rigid about.

I'm also balancing the use of these terms against the risk of antagonising the increasing separation between "insiders" and "outsiders" in our society. This isn't my intention as I'd primarily like to show how people at different degrees of separation can be useful and synergistic to eachother, but for want of better terms, I will continue with these. Perhaps a future edition will include someone's suggestions of a better phrasing to avoid this problem.

This is the map in its most general form. There are lots of ways we can scale & adapt the map to make it more specific. In the ABCD context, it would be possible to replace "external" with "institutions" and "internal" with "community", and indeed, we will do so throughout this book for ease. But it also works well at the level of the individual, where "internal" is the individual and "external" is anyone else, and, coming from a background in healthcare, it maps well onto different health interventions we attempt to carry out at the individual level.

From a scale of nations, we can also see traditional national colonialism as changes defined & carried out by outside nations inside other nations. The common theme here is that of being internal or external to a particular system - be that an individual, a community or a nation - and understanding that, as scales of systems are nested within each other, the changes can be defined in similar ways.

Order of Effects

Inspired by Ivan Illich's method, for each of the four roads of the Helper's Crossroads, we're going to examine effects that occur on five different levels. Each level is an "order of effect" because it is built on the accumulation of changes that occur in the previous levels.

The first order is the "Task-level" which is concerned with whether the task is achieved. In most cases, the same "task" can be achieved successfully by following any of the four roads. However, what is different is what happens at the higher levels. Within this order, we're also going to consider whether the task that was set was actually the right one, and the immediate consequences of it not being so (e.g. side-effects & waste).

The second order is the "Person-level" which is concerned with the effects on the person who is the object of the task, whether this is someone who is "helped" by another or the person helping themselves. This is the first order at which "side-effects" accumulate. Illich called this "personal iatrogenesis".

The third order is the "Community-level", which is concerned with the effects that are visible on the level of communities when citizens that make them up begin to change on the second level. Illich called this level "social iatrogenesis".

The fourth order is the "Cultural-level", which is concerned with what changes manifest in culture when many communities accumulate changes in the third level. Illich called this "cultural iatrogenesis".

The final order we will consider is the "Institutional-level", which is the effect that changes in culture have on institutions, and professionals that work within them. It is the feedback effects felt by institutions when they try to help in certain ways.

It is extremely important to consider all five orders of effect when deciding *how* to help someone. In contrast, most planning occurs only considering the first, and sometimes the second level. I've seen very little go beyond two orders of effect. In not connecting the mode of helping with its order of effects, many of the problems that manifest at higher orders of effects, especially the 5th Order (institutional level), appear to come out of thin air. Thus, this usually ends up being attributed to either bad "customers" or bad professionals. One of the purposes of this book is to link back these problems to the mode of helping employed by a logical professional.

It is important to note that this segregation isn't always clear cut, one effect can really span multiple orders and often, the order of effects can reinforce back down the levels. For example, the To/For mode of helping, by causing harm on the personal level to many people, can cause harm on the cultural level. This cultural harm can actually then magnify the effects of the harm on the personal level. Therefore don't become too hung up on which "order" a particular effect belongs to, they are only a method of illustration.

Chapter 4:
The "To/For" Road

As discussed in the Introduction, the "To/For" road is almost the default mode of helping that we see in our society. In other places, we call the "For" road "charity", "paternalism", "white saviour syndrome" in the international context or even "the nanny state". Meanwhile, we call the "To" road "corruption", "exploitation" or "imperialism". This is the road that almost all helpers walk down at some point, simply because it's where we're all directed. Sometimes it's necessary, often it's not. We'll discuss later why both "To" and "For" are considered together.

Using our map, we can understand that this road is defined as one in which:

- An outsider primarily defines the problem & the solution
- The solution primarily uses the outsider's resources.

For example:

- A doctor's diagnosis of a disease with a referral for surgery/medication
- A Local Authority who pays someone to go into various communities and find places that will benefit from a new general "Get into work" scheme they've devised with the help of specialists.
- Anyone performing a "Needs Assessment" in a community where the needs are pre-defined or limited and the intention is that they'll solve those problems on their behalf
- An NGO arriving in an overseas community handing out food imported from abroad
- A Public Health body seeks to remedy the lack of green spaces in an area, a social determinant of health, by selecting a site, paying money to contractors to create a community garden with no local involvement
- Funders who give money to organisations conditional on reporting on particular outcomes
- Any remedy to fix "health" as defined by a person/ other than the person to whom the "health" belongs.

Even in conventional wisdom, we intuitively understand how some of these interventions might go: for example, medical misdiagnosis, delayed diagnosis of something that was clearer to those within the family unit, or sayings like "they don't know what it's really like to live here". Less commonly do we recognise how many interventions that we see around us share similar characteristics.

A further point to note is that by examining these interventions through an objective framework, we bypass the conventional moral one that puts these mistakes down to "bad" doctors or "bad" professionals, thus requiring better training, better policies, better accountability etc. If we recognise that this has nothing to do with the "bad" professional, but with objective criteria like who defines the problem and who solves it, we can see that more training, more policies and more accountability do little to change this reality. We are not pointing out misdiagnosis by institutions as a problem to be solved by better institutions, but by allowing self-diagnosis by communities themselves.

To/For Road Qualities

All roads can lead to the same outcome - for example, a bike being fixed (a first-order effect)- but *how* that outcome is achieved is associated with certain other characteristics that crop up again and again (a second-order effect). For the To/For road, these are:

1st Order - Task-level

- The task solves the wrong problem, leading to side effects without the balance of benefit, and waste
- Unanticipated side-effects
- Potential for abuse of power, exploitation & corruption (To vs. For)

2nd Order - Person-level

- Dependence
- Person internalises a negative, powerless self-image
- The person becomes "labelled" out of community, especially where there is the reinforcement of cultural credentialism
- Resistance

3rd Order - Community-level

- Displacement of community mechanisms
- People end up segregated by labels, defined out of community and institutionalised
- Group dependence

4th Order - Cultural-level

- Credentialism
- Institutionalisation of helping
- Cultural Resistance

5th Order - Institutional-level

- Spiralling demand
- Professional burnout
- Professional alienation
- Bureaucracy & risk aversion

I'm sure this list is not complete, and people will continue to add to this list over time. We'll now discuss some of these in more detail.

1st Order - Task-Level

Solving the wrong problem

How many times have we all, in our lives, solved the wrong problem? In school exams, the direction to "Read the Question" is drilled into us, or perhaps we work on a particular negative aspect of our life, only to realise it was just a symptom of an underlying problem. In fact, we can see examples all around us where very very clever people spent an inordinate amount of time, energy, money & brainpower to solve a problem, but all the time, they were walking in the wrong direction.

There is much conventional wisdom around which directs us to first be sure we are walking in the right direction. Savvy farmers will observe for four consecutive seasons before planting a new field. In permaculture, the first principle of design is "observe & interact" in this vein. However, we often fail to see that at least some, if not many of the "problems" that institutions try to solve in our communities, or health professionals try to solve in our bodies, are simply the wrong problem. Further evidence of this is that when a series of professionals of diverse services look at the same person or community, they often find different problems to be the root cause (usually whichever one they are paid to fix!)

To find out why we often solve the wrong problem, it's necessary to take a brief trip into the deeps of the history of human knowledge & science. We are in the middle of a major transition from a mechanically-informed view of the world, where the functioning of the world is reducible, predictable and akin to clockwork, to a complexity-informed view of the world where the world is made up of diverse, interdependent and constantly changing components, the results of changes to which are difficult to predict.

All models are wrong, some are useful, and so there are plenty of things that are indeed reducible & predictable enough to be useful in this way. For example, man has (intellectually) made it to the moon with the use of pure Newtonian mechanics. However, problems arise when we continue to use poor mechanical models because we have failed to understand the complex (but not complicated) nature of a problem, and therefore try to solve the wrong problem. The unstated assumption in much community work is that all communities are basically the same, responding predictably to similar stimuli, and therefore that which works in one neighbourhood will work in another. Therefore, this is a good place to look at how we define communities & neighbourhoods, and the effect of these definitions on whether we choose to apply mechanical or complex models to problem solving.

Neighbourhood vs. Community

In neighbourhoods, the boundaries are arbitrary, and the neighbourhood is understood through mechanical, quantitative measures called "collective properties". Collective properties are aggregations of properties that belong to the individuals that make up the group, for example, average age, percentage unemployment or median income. From this perspective, if some people of the neighbourhood are expelled and replaced with different people who happen to have exactly the same demographic characteristics, the neighbourhood is assumed not to have changed, because the quantitative measures haven't changed.

Communities, however, are ecosystems of people. Their boundaries are defined by relationships and are often vague and imperceptible. They are composed not just of people and their properties, but of relationships and connections. In contrast to "collective properties", they are understood through qualities called "emergent properties" such as "welcoming", "friendly" or "safe". This network of relationships is always fluid and changing, and is very sensitive to small changes.

While institutions who operate with a mechanical world view see where we live as simply neighbourhoods, a complexity-informed view better reflects the way that we actually experience where we live (i.e. through our relationships to people and places, not through data). From this view arises the philosophy that underpins ABCD and other similar models.

It is through viewing communities through the lens of data and mechanics, thereby reducing them to neighbourhoods, that the idea that specialist experts, (i.e. accumulated knowledge & "education" within a single individual or a group of individuals) are better managers of the neighbourhood than those within the system without the specialist "education".

So often when institutions seek out problems and solutions, they look to what worked elsewhere. Experts note that where "X" was a problem in one neighbourhood, "Y" fixed it, and so experts in organising services lobby, secure funding and organise to find "X" in other neighbourhoods and do "Y" again. More experts are employed who are either experts at finding "X", implementing "Y", or both. Within the mechanical, neighbourhood perspective, this is a very logical thing to do, but I hope the assumptions this process is built on start to become clear so we can call them into question.

The truth is that communities are not predictable, clockwork systems but complex adaptive systems, and so the above model loses its usefulness. As Cormac Russell says "when you've seen one community, you've seen one community". Communities consist of a large number of individual citizens who act independently, but also adapt their actions to the community around them, and have relationships with other citizens within and without that community in an irregular pattern, which qualifies it as a Complex Adaptive System. That being so, we can learn from what is known about these systems in general.

For example, one thing that we know is common to all complex adaptive systems is that even very minor, almost imperceptible differences in the "current state" of a system can cause wildly different reactions to the same stimulus. In complexity speak, this is called "sensitivity to initial conditions".

All of this is why very clever people, with the best intentions, often choose the wrong goal to apply their clever solutions to. They see communities as a collection of data, missing all the things that make it unique and all the subtle differences in the current state that wildly change the outcome.

My personal favourite example of this is "We Can't Eat a Road" (Yeneabat and Butterfield, 2012)[2], a story of an NGO pursuing their goal, not the community's. However, there are plenty of other examples that I'm sure you'll recognise from your life where an outsider pursued or recommended the wrong goal based on ignorance of the particulars. I often think back to Michael Gove's famous "people have had enough of experts", and think it was an extremely astute observation of the general consensus on experts' ability to choose the right problem.

So, we've set out here why those outside the system struggle to define the problem. We'll revisit this subject in later chapters from the opposite perspective, why those internal to the system are the experts.

Unanticipated Side Effects

From the same conditions that gave rise to "solving the wrong problem" also arise "unanticipated side effects". When both combine, the scales tip even further towards

---

[2] Yeneabat, M and Butterfield, A.K. (2012) ""We Can't Eat a Road:" Asset-Based Community Development and The Gedam Sefer Community Partnership in Ethiopia" *Journal of Community Practice* (20:1-2) pp. 134-153 Doi: 10.1080/10705422.2012.650121

the harm that wasn't anticipated as there is no benefit to balance it, but each can arise independently too.

It appears that harming-by-helping is more recognised in medicine (with concepts such as iatrogenesis, harm vs. benefit and pharmacological side effects) than in the wider helping world, and so, it is rare in medicine to find interventions that are done "just because there's no harm in it". Meanwhile, this doesn't appear to be the case in certain other professional & community spheres. For example, we might hear "why not set up a community garden in every neighbourhood? What harm could it do?"

One of the central themes of ABCD, and what sets it apart from other models, is the recognition that these are not harmless interventions.

Systems are complex and full of interdependencies, adaptations and relationships that are hidden to almost everyone. Unlike a clock or even a complicated (but not complex[3]) space rocket, those acting from the outside based on data cannot map out a large complex system's current state to a degree that enables us to take account

---

[3] A space rocket is *complicated* because it is made up of a very large number of individual parts, but it is still reducible to a mechanical model in the same as your car. It's not *complex* because those parts are not individual actors that interrelate in almost unpredictable ways and adapt to eachother, like a school or an ant colony does.

of "sensitivity to initial conditions" and thus understand how an external stimulus will affect this state.

Meanwhile, those people inside the system are subject to direct feedback from it every single day. Just as a regular driver of a vehicle will notice a subtle change in engine noise much earlier than someone who rarely drives the vehicle, the subtle and early appearance of these side effects are felt first by those who get the most holistic, consistent and direct feedback from the system on a daily basis - those who make up the system.

It's not that these side effects don't manifest clearly in some way, but that outsiders are removed from sensing these side effects, and they wouldn't be looking for them even if they weren't. Long before there is any change in quantitative data, early changes are often purely qualitative. Residents will say "I just can't put my finger on it" or "it doesn't feel the same". Being just the unquantifiable experiences of "non-expert" people, if this feedback even makes its way back to the outsiders, it is usually ignored. But just as when early signs of disease are ignored, it will manifest later with more obvious, measurable but serious problems, so too do the side effects of the "wrong problem" usually only become obvious to the outsiders when it's far too late and the damage is done. That is, if they are actually still listening and haven't already packed their bags and gone home patting each other on the back for a job well done.

Of course, there are not only the task-specific side-effects, but all the concepts I discuss in this book could be considered "side effects" too. All too often, these are ignored for the same reason - they are not measurable, and therefore are assumed to have no impact on the community. I hope to use this book to make these qualities more explicit, noticeable and valued.

So, when an outsider defines the problem, not only are they prone to defining the wrong goal, but when they do, they have unintended, harmful, side effects that are not counterbalanced by other benefits. This should be seen as an occupational hazard of trying to help from the outside. This is in opposition to the general trend to lay these effects at the feet of individual helpers who get the blame for being apparently incompetent or immoral. This book is not to bash professionals & specialists, but to free them from the rock & the hard place they are caught between: forced to use the "To/For" road by the system, with all its risks, but personally accountable for when those risks go wrong. When we understand that they are outsiders trying their best, we must therefore expect less than perfect decisions. The solution is not to beat professionals into unachievable perfect models, but to limit our exposure to those things where we really cannot do without professionals, where the benefits outweigh the risks.

Why do we assume that the outsider knows better than the insider?

The "outsider defines the goal" row of the model, and its subsequent roads (To, For & Through), are far more common than the "insider-defined" row. The reason for this runs very deep indeed. The next few paragraphs are a brief attempt to trace the intellectual history of this thought but can be skipped if uninterested or, if you don't agree, they are not pivotal to the argument.

The idea that situations faced by humanity are best managed by the few "clever people", by expertise derived from education (or revelation through being chosen) rather than coal-face experience; the idea that people are "wild" and "emotional" and need to be kept in check by their "rational" "betters"; and that "common sense is not so common" has threaded its way through much of western philosophy, from Plato's Republic and Socrates' theory of knowledge to Stoicism and Capitalism (i.e. the invisible hand of the market puts economic power in the hands of the most competent), as well as in arguments against universal suffrage and even in the fundamental assumptions of representative democracy.

But if we begin with the principles that proximity to a situation grants an expertise that education cannot match (as I do here), and/or that people have the competency and capacity to deal with them, then the ensuing arguments are extremely challenging ideas to almost all dominant paradigms, structures and systems of power. This is why ABCD is so radical.

It is in this way that we give up much of our freedom by believing the very myth they feed us: that we are not competent to define our own problem and we couldn't solve it well even if we did. We hand power over our lives to professionals, specialists, governments and large businesses, on the assumption that we cannot do what they do. Having handed over this power, we then create (largely ineffective) systems of "accountability" (e.g. professional or statutory regulatory bodies, civil law, complaints departments, etc.) to attempt to ensure that those we have handed our power over to wield it in our best interest (which also creates new problems in itself i.e. risk aversion), rather than question why we handed over this power in the first place.

"To" vs. "For"

Often there are only subtle differences between the "To" and the "For" roads. The distinction I make in this model is to whom the benefits of any change primarily accrue. On the "To" road, the solution prescribed by an outsider is actually to benefit the outsider. Often we call the "To" road "imperialism". We also tend to regulate against it in certain professions ("exploitation") or even criminalise it ("corruption"). Certainly, in many instances, it looks like exploitation and is socially unacceptable. For example:

- When healthcare professionals choose a treatment option that is not necessarily the best option for the patient, but is the least likely to result in legal action. For example, for a paramedic, taking a patient to hospital "just in case" (where there is a high risk of infection) even when it's not required because it's safer for their job than leaving them at home (clinician-centred healthcare).
- When GPs are incentivised to diagnose a disease in a population that makes no functional difference to the person.
- When healthcare systems prioritise their own needs over the needs of a population (system-centred healthcare).
- A business enforcing worse terms & conditions on a workforce.
- An NGO who enters a situation because it's attractive to volunteers willing to pay, leading to "profit" as paid wages to upper echelon staff
- Nations colonially dictating to other nations
- A politician taking bribes to enforce a particular change

On the other hand, on the "For" road, the solution prescribed by the outsider is (primarily, and in reality) in the benefit of the internal system. We usually call this "Charity", "Philanthropy" or "Paternalism" and it is socially encouraged. The original list under the heading "To/For" serves as an example list for "For", and I'm sure we're all familiar enough with "charity" to need no further explanation.

However, despite the completely different perception (socially unacceptable "To" vs socially encouraged "For"), they both share two critical features: the goal is set by the outsider and uses outside resources. Furthermore, as seen above, while there are many legitimate "For" efforts by genuinely well-intentioned people, as well as many "To" changes that don't hide behind any pretence, much of "To" actually masquerades as "For". For example:

- The NGO justifies its mission as to help the situation, even if the unconscious primary driver and primary (or only) beneficiaries are the NGO itself
- The healthcare professionals justify their decision as being in the interests of patient safety, such as "rather be safe than sorry".
- Nations saying they are "bringing democracy" to another nation

Perceptions of whether an intervention is "To" or "For" can also change over time. Gay Conversion Therapy and the Electric Shock Therapy were considered to be in the benefit of the person ("For") at the time, but most people would now agree that they were "To" (where benefits accrued to those interested in maintaining a particular cultural status quo or those who financially profited from such therapies). What else do we consider to be in the person's interests now that will we look back on with horror?[4].

We already implicitly recognise that "To" & "For" are dangerously similar because we regulate so heavily to avoid that outcome. Regulation of institutions and professionals is one of the ways society attempts to ensure that they remain on the "For" road and don't move over to the "To" road. When the head of a charity is found to be in receipt of large pay-offs, there is a huge scandal in the media. Often one hears complaints at what the CEOs of NGOs or charities are paid, where they're seen to be personally benefiting from the situation.

Once again, the traditional thinking is that the problem is a moral debasement of society or lack of regulation, so the only solution proposed is that we need stronger incentives (morals) to stay on the "For" road and disincentives (regulation, law) to crossing over to the "To" road. When we look at the whole crossroads, however, we can see there is another solution; to recognise that "To" and "For" are so close that it is extremely easy for anyone on those roads to begin, even unconsciously, working towards their own ends rather than others, even through just being subject to societal biases - e.g. homophobia in the late 20th Century and fatphobia now.

---

[4] For what it's worth, I personally think we'll look back in horror at our current discourse around weight, diet & exercise.

The need to ensure that those to whom we give the power to act in our interests - the "For" road - do not actually use it to their own benefit - the "To" road - is the material driver of accountability, and in turn, risk aversion, bureaucracy and ultimately, burnout. We'll cover these in the Institutional-level.

2nd Order - Personal-level

<u>Dependence</u>

There are two ways that dependence is created. The first is physical, through the altering of the material reality; the second psychological, through the adaptation of someone's psychology to the new material reality.

When an institution enters a person's life, normally at the point someone receives a label like "at-risk youth", "frail" or "lonely", suddenly a professional shows up in their life with a powerful and invasive relationship. This displaces the other relationships in someone's life and weakens other "coping mechanisms" that might have existed in their family or community network. This is something that isn't often considered and mitigated for: the very presence of a professional in a person's life is disruptive.

For example, a non-labelled person might have a strong network of friends who support their mental health

("With" relationships). But when they receive a diagnosis such as "personality disorder" or such like, they usually also begin to develop relationships with professionals, like a therapist, a GP or a mental health crisis line ("To/For" relationships"). What is implied here in the giving of a diagnostic label and treatment by an institution is that they have a problem that can only be fixed by the institution, with the person and their support network taking a purely supportive role led by the institution (now "Through" relationships"). In this material reality, it is only natural that the relationship between the person and their support network weakens, as the "problem" gets taken to the institution who has promised to provide experts to make them "better" rather than the supposedly unqualified friends who are supposed to know less than the experts.

It is in this way that the presence of an institution in someone's life can displace and weaken other coping mechanisms that previously existed in their life and community. This is only accounting for the way that the person chooses to use the options available to them, and later we'll talk about how the presence of a label also causes the relationships to weaken from the other end out of "credentialism".

And so, having turned up in someone's life, implied they have a problem that only the institution can fix, displaced their other coping mechanisms, institutions and professionals are then surprised when a "service user" has no other option but to use their services to solve other (often related) problems the institution doesn't consider appropriate. On a large scale, this is what is driving the crisis of demand in the NHS.

This is even more extreme when we take away someone's freedom, either by imprisonment or sectioning, where we are *specifically & purposefully* excluding them from their community and decimating their relationships, either in "their interest" or "in the interest of society". Is it any surprise, therefore, that when allowed to rejoin their community, their social ties have decayed and they have no choice but to turn to institutions for help?

Following the physical altering of reality, there is also a resulting psychological adaptation. Of course, this is to be expected if we realise that our own internal models of our reality are constantly adjusting to the reality around us. So, if our reality is changed from one where, alongside others in our community, we contribute and cooperate in an equitable way ("By" & "With"), to one where we are passive receivers of charity ("To/For" & "Through"), stopped from contributing to our own solutions, isolated from our neighbours and known by our diagnostic labels, then, of course, our self-image will also change from one of positive, confident interdependence to negative, unconfident, powerless dependence.

Alongside obvious examples of institutionalisation of prisoners & long term patients in hospitals (e.g. long term section orders), I have seen this process play out personally many times in other areas. From the refugees who arrived on the island of Lesbos as triumphant survivors but then began rapidly to see themselves as powerless victims (the same way as the services around them saw them), to healthcare patients who, on receiving a medical diagnosis of a long-term condition (necessitating increased contact with health services), start to become institutionalised by the health system. This even goes so far as being rewarded for being "compliant", "looking after themselves" and "helping themselves", which is often tantamount to just following the doctor's orders, and berated for the opposite (the issue of whether an elderly person should remain in their home or move to a care home is an example where this contradiction becomes really clear. Also, consider the loaded phrase "not looking after themselves").

In this latter example, we can see that institutionalisation can also be an active process, not just a passive one, as "service users" are rewarded for compliance - even if that's only through a more pleasant demeanour and a compliment on how well they're looking after themselves - and "punished" for non-compliance - from subtle disapproving looks to full tellings-off.

Another prism through which to see this journey to dependence is Berne's Transactional Analysis (TA). In short, the theory is that there are three roles we can play in any interaction: parent, child and adult. There are two stable pairs - parent-child and adult-adult - and two unstable pairs - parent-adult and child-adult. If an interaction starts in an unstable pairing, then it will collapse into one of the stable ones.

To note here, I'm not a fan of using the language "parent, adult, child" because it feels demeaning. I think we could replace this with "helper" or "provider" instead of "parent", "citizen" instead of "adult" and "paternalistic receiver" or "consumer" instead of "child". For brevity and to keep with terms that those familiar with TA will be used to, I will continue using those terms with this caveat.

As an adult, relationships with others in the neighbourhood are naturally adult-adult, whereas the relationship with an institution is rarely adult-adult, it's normally parent-child. Approaching an institution as an "adult", with the institution approaching their service users as a "parent" (paternalistically), means the relationship must be forced towards a stable pairing. The citizen is thus trained by the institution to act as a "child" - i.e. follow without question orders by their beneficent carers. One can see the threat that "adult-adult" relationships pose to institutions by just asking your local health care professionals whether they like treating other health care professionals (who naturally approach as an 'institutional insider' and more "adult").

Psychological dependence can become really visible when an institutional helper tries to approach an institutionalised person as an "adult" once more, but the person has been trained not to relate as an "adult" or as an equal partner/citizen and cannot simply return to acting the "adult" role in that context easily (N.B. this doesn't mean they are unable to act the "adult" role in other contexts).

In this situation, I've then seen these professionals quickly write this person off as simply unwilling to take responsibility for themselves, further reinforcing the idea that professionals are required to do things "For" this dependent person. Scaled up, we see this narrative transformed into "the scrounging class" vs. the "taxpayer" or other such adaptations. This is a self-reinforcing paradigm as these professionals do not note that it was the institution and the professionals themselves who created the dependence in the first place.

Finally, this process is a reinforcing cycle: the arrival into someone's life, if done incorrectly, can precipitate a decay in their community connections and replace informal ways of dealing with problems. From then, reduced community capacity to deal with a problem means an institution is used to solve it instead, further strengthening the person's relationship to the institution and weakening their relationships to others, diminishing further their capacity to find their solutions in their community, and so on.

Labelled out of community

In order for institutions to work efficiently, labels like "unemployed", "mentally ill" or "diabetic" are applied to people, which direct which professional they will see and what interventions are likely to work to help them. This is a fairly logical thing to do when you want to be efficient and leverage "specialism" and economy of scale, but there are those who push back against these labels for various reasons - be that association with prejudice, the lack of similarity between people currently under one label, or the fight for the right to receive a label from an institution.

These are all valid but are beyond the scope of this book as many others have written great pieces of literature on the problems of labels, better than anything I could write. Therefore, here, I want to look mainly at the effects of the labelling process, particularly on the community.

When a label is applied by an institution, it is almost like they are stamping ownership on a person, a stamp which tells all other would-be helpers that this person has problems that can't possibly be dealt with by anyone except a professional (otherwise, why would the institution be involved?). So, some family members and neighbours tend to be put off from interfering too much in the professional's plan for the labelled person. The transfer of authority for decision making from the person to the professional is reinforced by others. This is magnified when someone is solely known in their community by their label, rather than by their gifts.

This is a microcosm of "credentialism" which we'll discuss later, and the culture of credentialism magnifies this effect at the personal level.

To put it most simply, labelling someone out of community is the way that the person's ability to find help in their family or neighbourhood to achieve self-defined goals ("With") is diminished by the carrying of an institutional label - and this is on top of any stigma that comes with particular labels such as "HIV" or "Tuberculosis", which has a similar effect.

Instead of it being assumed by the people around the labelled person that they have the agency to decide what is best for them, they now ask "what would your doctor/social worker say about that? Perhaps you should ask them first?", and feeling hesitant to help (at least with certain things) without the professional's approval.

Resistance

I think many others have summed up how they feel about organisations practising "To/For" help much better than I can. For example, Lilla Watson says:

"If you have come here to help me, you are wasting your time. But if you have come because your liberation is bound up with mine, then let us work together."

And Cormac Russell put it well when he said that when change is done to people, it is felt as violence. Indeed, it is really a violation.

An oft-heard exclamation by helpers is "it's like they just don't want our help". Indeed, resistance to being helped isn't an uncommon phenomenon, and is normally called "non-compliance" or being a "difficult patient". This is true in health systems, NGOs or even in the military about the "liberation" of places like Iraq.

Much of the discourse around human rights, the "small state" vs. the "nanny state" and liberal democracy is resistance to the "To/For" mode. The truth is that we all initially resist people coming into our lives and telling us what to do. That is, until we are ground down into being "compliant", as if the good life is one where you always do what specialists tell you.

3rd Order - Community-level

Dependence

Communities are essentially networks that help citizens meet their needs, at least in part. Community members use the community gift economy to flatten out the peaks and troughs of various resources (e.g. of income). Imagine a community that has a decentralised & complex way of growing food for everyone. The net result over many years of evolution is that certain houses grow certain foodstuffs in the right quantity, and in a complex community ritual, those foodstuffs are swapped and exchanged in the right quantities. In periods of isolated poor harvests (e.g. one garden's tomatoes are decimated by blight), not only does everyone remain fed, but the community bonds actually grow in response.

However, when new actors enter that system that meet those needs in a different way, those networks & ways of meeting needs can decay. In this hypothetical example, a supermarket, unannounced and uninvited, opens up in the town, deciding it can create efficiency & value for money (even though this wasn't a problem the community wanted to solve) and begins supplying all foods anyone in the community could ever want at any time and cheaper. Those citizens start to grow a relationship between them and the supermarket, while their relationship to each other starts to decay. The community, over time, forgets that they ever *could* grow food for themselves.

Now their critical need - food - is met in only one way. In times of poor harvest far away or other crises, the supermarket starts to empty. Whereas previously, crises strengthened bonds in an antifragile way, now crises in the supermarket lead to hoarding and fights over packets of rice. The elders and the spokesmen wonder why the "morals" of the community, of the younger generation, have been lost. It has nothing to do with morals, but changes in material reality.

The supermarket decides one day, all of a sudden, unilaterally, that it's no longer profitable to operate in this community, so they shut up shop. Crisis ensues. Some community members lobby the supermarket to re-open. Some lobby the government to open a nationalised government supermarket. Some beg philanthropists for the money to set up their own supermarket. But a few others remember stories of when they used to create food for themselves, without a supermarket or any outside help; however, the work of reweaving these connections is intensive. While this latter is the best option for sustainability, antifragility, resilience and community cohesion - the "By" road - it obviously would have been better if the supermarket just hadn't had the hubris & arrogance to open in the first place.

This story is an allegory for what is happening across communities throughout the whole world, and most advanced in industrialised, western countries.

More and more institutions - be they large businesses, government departments or charities - are "setting up shop" in our communities (often uninvited, to solve non-existent problems they often haven't been asked to solve, mainly to justify their own continued existence and employment). When they do so, they unknowingly change the shape of the system in which they're working from one that involves lots of complex interdependencies between neighbours to one that is one directional.

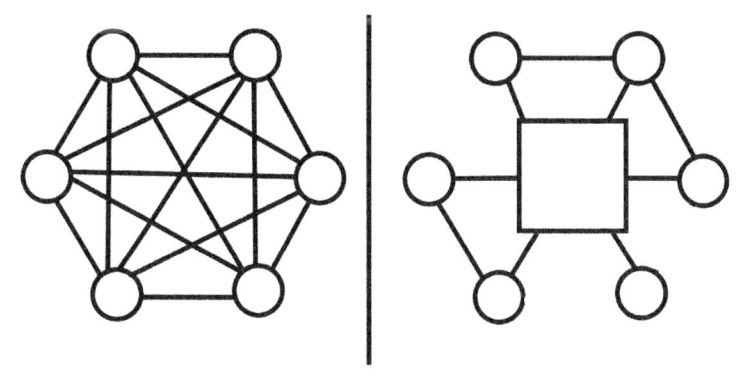

(Fig 3.) - Left: Nodes are well inter-connected to each other individual node. Right: Nodes are less inter-connected, as they connect through a central, influential node.

Every "service" set up by an institution is a shop that has this same effect, and is the same whether it's an NGO turning up in a village abroad or a charity starting to work in a new neighbourhood at home. The net result is the same. Disruption and dependence.

Then, when funding dries up, business "calls for difficult decisions", there is a change in administration or when 'austerity is the agenda of the day, and the relationship on which the community now depends is removed, the system is thrown into chaos. The community cannot instantly take back over those functions in the same way that they could before.

Let me state this clearly. Organisations often think that, by getting funding for a year, then that means they should do good for one year, even if they cannot get funding for subsequent years. This is not the case. By being present in the community, you have altered that system, and it is most unethical to create reliance and then to leave the system in disarray.

Another way to visualise this is through natural systems. When we start to "manage" an area of land, we disrupt the natural ecosystem of plants. But when we stop intervening in that land, perhaps thinking we are "rewilding", the land will not suddenly return to its pre-managed state. Instead, the most invasive species of plant - for example, brambles - will take over, whereas previously the land was wildflower meadow. That is abandonment, not rewilding. Rewilding takes careful, energy-intensive input to recreate a natural, sustainable ecosystem. What many institutions are doing when they leave a community is not "rewilding", but abandonment.

Any decision to take the "To/For" road should consider this effect, plan how to keep damage to community relations to a minimum and simultaneously plan and create provisions for "rewilding" in the event of shutting up shop, along the line of the principle "leave no trace".

But currently, this is almost totally overlooked when using this mode of helping.

4th Order - Cultural-level

<u>Credentialism</u>

Previously we discussed how those around a person react when they get a label and come under the "care of" an institution. When scaled up, what we see is a culture of credentialism, and this is what we're now seeing across our communities: a reluctance to help neighbours for lack of credentials, out of fear of doing the wrong thing. This isn't helped by the influence of the "Through" road either, which we'll discuss in a later chapter. The myths of the institutional system - that only those with specialist training are able to help - has seeped through into the community.

In a culture of credentialism, even before labelling, those who are best placed to help when needed, in a "With" way, are actually hesitant to help. As previously discussed, neighbours and friends become hesitant to talk about mental health because they're not "suicide first-aid trained" or "qualified to talk about mental health", when all that is needed is an attentive ear. So instead, people are pointed towards web chats and hotlines run by "trained volunteers" and institutions with professionals.

Similarly, whereas previously problems with young children were dealt with by the wisdom of mothers & grandmothers in the community, the media, the justice system and the risk-averse health system have created a culture where only a (senior[5]) healthcare professional is qualified to say that everything is okay in. A&Es are overwhelmed with parents looking for simple advice that would have been easily found amongst fellow mothers & grandmothers a few decades ago. In a culture of credentialism, those same mothers & grandmothers now feel "unqualified" and say they should get the child checked out by the GP/A&E/999 "just in case" there is a rare medical cause. This is a byproduct of institutional care, not a failure of mother's to take responsibility, which is the usual institutional line.

Another great example is the way the ambulance service and the health service more generally, over many years, have insisted on an assessment of an elderly person who has fallen over "just in case", which has influenced the culture. Now, people are scared to pick up their elderly neighbour off the floor in case they've injured themself (despite the fact the person on the floor is telling them nothing is wrong), and instead waiting 12 hours for an ambulance service to do so, who are busy picking up everyone else in the same situation.

---

[5] In the UK this has been de facto narrowed to GPs and paediatric emergency consultants due to the highly litigious culture. Many ambulance services now have a policy to take all under 1 year old's to an A&E, regardless of the severity of the concern.

This happens across many different aspects of life, with the institution creating a rod for its own back.

These are just a few examples from my own experience in the ambulance service - the neighbours who feel they can't pick up a neighbour off the floor because they haven't been medically trained, a listening ear to their friends going through a hard time because they haven't been trained in suicide prevention, they can't help a fellow mother to quieten a crying baby in case they miss a rare medical cause.

But there are more. Someone who is deemed "vulnerable" by an institution is only culturally allowed to interact with people with, or under the supervision of someone with, a DBS certificate, or people who have been "safeguarding" trained. This prevents genuine diversity in the community.
The culture of credentialism is a product of institutions and is driving a huge amount of the demand it is struggling with.

The institutionalisation of helping culture

Whereas the culture of credentialism is the hesitance of neighbours to lend an informal hand out of fear of legal consequences or doing the wrong thing, the institutionalisation of helping culture is the way that the people with the problem themselves begin to look to institutions for the good life. The work of John McKnight, in particular in "The Careless Society", as well as

Cormac Russell, carefully documents the way that culture has shifted to looking to the institution for "the Good Life", and I don't intend to repeat too much here, as it has already been said better than I could explain.

Cultural Resistance - "We've had enough of experts"

Michael Gove, a senior UK government minister, said in 2016 "I think the people of this country have had enough of experts, with organisations with acronyms saying that they know what is best and getting it consistently wrong". I watched as many of my professional colleagues and fellow inhabitants of the left side of politics howled in indignation. They just couldn't believe that anyone could agree with him.

I think the evidence points in Gove's favour, however. Firstly we must address that many minority groups have very strong, valid reasons to distrust institutions. For example, institutions have policed LGBT relationships and attempted to forcibly "cure" people of their sexuality, and institutions still act as gatekeepers of people's official gender identities, and the misuse of this power has been fatal. Black people have been forcibly used for medical experiments such as the perfection of the science of gynaecology as well as the infamous Tuskegee Syphilis Study. Even today, the current obsession with "obesity" has its roots in, and still disproportionately targets, people of colour. Institutions stop and search black people in the UK nineteen times more, and institutions regularly murder black people in the USA. In Australia, Aboriginal families have been ripped apart by institutions who forcibly removed aboriginal children from their families to be "Australianised". The list goes on of the ways that institutions have previously done "To" certain minority groups.

A professional reading this will reply, quite validly, that this isn't them doing this, and they'd be right in most cases. I'm a paramedic by trade, and have never practised gynaecology on black slaves or removed an aboriginal child or stopped and searched someone. It might be a completely different professional or a completely different country, or happened before they were born. But here it is not facts that matter, but perception. It is institutions in general, from the state to the health service, who are distrusted. This is one driver for mistrust.

However, there is also growing distrust in institutions amongst non-minority groups. This is what Michael Gove - a white, upper-class male - was really referring to when he said "people". These people are experiencing "To" and even "For" and learning, through experience, the qualities of that road. Gove specifically referred to a point we've previously mentioned: "the wrong problem".

This mistrust is manifesting in more subtle ways than Michael Gove coming on TV and bashing professionals trying their best, however. Even before the pandemic, conspiracy theories & "Fake News" were a cause for concern, driving racial violence and even terrorism. The anti-vax movement had also caused a resurgence of measles in the USA.

During the COVID-19 pandemic, these contradictions really came to the fore, however. Significant groups of the population didn't believe the virus existed, mistrusted the intentions of the lockdown, accused health care professionals of being complicit, refused to wear masks and campaigned against the vaccine. Unsurprisingly, communities with longstanding and historic mistrust in institutions tended to be more hesitant about the vaccine (though notably were not primary instigators of anti-vax/COVID/mask campaigns).

The traditional response to these people from non-COVID sceptics is disbelief and labelling. However, it doesn't take too much thinking to realise that this is driven by mistrust in institutions. It also doesn't take too much thinking to uncover the reasons for this mistrust. A few examples amongst many:

- Working-class communities were destroyed in return for promised "trickle-down" riches that never appeared.
- The war on Iraq, which is widely perceived to be because of oil and not of "Weapons of Mass Destruction" as originally purported.
- The banks were bailed out in the 2008 Financial Crisis, and the country has since undergone austerity, further devastating communities,

especially those in Scotland, Wales, Cornwall and the North of England.
- The UK "MP Expenses" scandal
- WikiLeaks, Panama Papers etc. uncovering government & economic corruption
- The Liberal Democrats U-turn on university tuition fees which scarred a generation of young people
- "£350 million for the NHS" in the event of Brexit, which hasn't yet appeared at the time of writing.

These are all government actions because they are the most obvious, but this is just the tip of the iceberg. The reality is that all institutions are tarred with the same brush.

The solution to mistrust is not belittling, patronising, labelling and definitely not force. Institutions can grow trust by putting their power back into communities, by lifting up and supporting community efforts, and by being seen to be responsible when they try to help, while communities can reconnect to welcome people back from the labelled edge.

5th Order - Institutional-level

Accountability

Because we think there is no alternative to the "To/For" road, we are always developing sophisticated systems to ensure that those invested with power stay on the "For" road. For example, in the health space, we have professional regulation, complaints systems, legal structures to "sue" and insurance to deal with the fallout. Parallel structures exist in many professions, institutions and organisations. Many community campaigns and institutional reform really only seek to tinker with these accountability structures for marginal gains in the integrity of the "For" road.

Much of the theory behind these accountability structures is to weed out the "bad apples", and for the rest, try to create some "skin in the game". For example, the theory goes that a doctor with no accountability will take advantage of their patients, but by introducing financial penalties through being sued or by losing their job, they have "skin in the game" and they will not exploit their patients[6]. Cleverly, however, each failure of the regulatory system to prevent exploitation becomes an argument for its strengthening, rather than

---

[6] Apparently, in the eyes of regulators and those that promote further regulation, this is the only reason professionals don't exploit their patients , ignoring that professionals are on the whole extremely caring people.

questioning whether it actually does what we think it does. Certainly, I want my heart surgeon to act in my best interests, and I certainly would like racists to be excluded from the list of my potential helpers. However, the solution is not to maximise regulation but to minimise exposure. Another reason for this is the side effects of overregulation.

Overregulation

Analysis of overregulation is pretty common in right-wing narratives ("too much red tape") but is almost non-existent in left-wing ones, probably because much of left-wing discourse is about growing institutions, not community.

Overregulation has very real effects. I think that the theory that giving helpers "skin in the game" is the best, only, or even just a good way to induce them to act in the person's best interests is incorrect. If anything, it is quite the opposite. It means that they do whatever they can to minimise their "skin in the game", even at the expense of the person being helped, leading to *more* "To", not less. The bias is not *towards* things that maximise the person's interests, but *away* from obvious harms *towards* subtle ones.

An example from my own world, the ambulance service: our job revolves mainly around the decision of whether to take someone to the hospital or to leave someone at home. The phrases heard everywhere are "I won't lose my job for taking the patient to hospital" or "I think the patient can stay at home, but I'm not willing to bet my mortgage". But taking someone to the hospital may well be more dangerous for the patient than leaving them at home. They may have only very minor injuries, like a skin tear, but in hospital, they are exposed to hospital-acquired infections, deconditioning, and in some cases, abuse.

If a patient were to be left at home and a very rare complication occurred (perhaps they got an infection in their skin tear, followed by sepsis and death), the paramedic's practice would be called into question. They might be sued or lose their job. But if that patient dies as a result of a hospital-acquired infection or some other side effect of being admitted to the hospital, not only will their practice not be called into question, they will probably never even know.

So, the patient safety agenda does not actually reduce harm to patients, it just shifts those harms away from ones for which the clinician or the institution might be sued or subject to disciplinary action, and towards harms for which they will not. Similar stories can be found in most professions according to the stories I've heard, but this is the scenario with which I'm most familiar so it works as an example. I've heard many professionals begging for trust and deregulation so that they can actually practice in the interests of the person they help, along with very valid concerns from citizens about what this would mean. The solution, again, is not deregulation or more regulation, but minimising exposure.

For a professional helper, this constant worry about accountability is also a huge driver of burnout, which we will discuss shortly.

The threat of accountability also changes the shape of institutions too. Bureaucracy is a state of an institution where risk is spread out across an organisation in such a way that no one person can be held responsible for a particular failing; it is a self-defence mechanism. We know that another property of bureaucracy is painfully slow reactions or ability to change. It also creates a risk-averse organisation, minimising its own financial exposure at the expense of the populations it attempts to serve. This is well known by professionals, who will straight away recognise the winning side in a conflict between an institution's financial liability and a person's best interests. The "red tape" that professionals complain is a barrier to good care is a reference to this issue.

In summary, beyond a certain point, systems of accountability do not prevent the "To" road, but **drive** it. It drives both clinicians and institutions to have no choice but to prioritise their interests over the person they're trying to help and to organise in ways that reduce risk rather than ways that work efficiently and responsively.

This chapter is not about bashing professionals or institutions. It is about the opposite. No helper I've ever personally met has bad intentions, we all just want to help, and many of us are frustrated by the barriers that are placed in our way, that we have no option but to respond to. This book is a manifesto for liberation from stress & burnout and from these barriers.

Spiralling demand

For a number of reasons previously discussed, from the culture of credentialism to creating dependence, one of the net effects of the "To/For" road is to create even more demand for the "To/For" road in future. It is a self-reinforcing loop.

Conservatives have been concerned about this spiralling demand for a long time, while liberals tend to ignore it or use it for arguments for more tax or nationalisation. This has led conservatives to argue for and implement austerity. The theory of this is that by reducing institutional budgets it will force services to contract and force community solutions to grow to replace them.

It is worth noting here that Asset-Based Community Development, as a result, is often accused of reinforcing these neoliberal narratives. This couldn't be further from the truth. We have to return to our natural systems analogy to explain why ABCD is not promoting austerity and why austerity as a solution to spiralling demand does not work.

Imagine a wildflower meadow on the edge of a wood, which can remain a pretty sustainable system for many years, crowding out invasive grasses as well as other invasive woodland border species such as brambles, feeding roaming herds of cattle and wildfowl. However, humans arrive and decide that they want to turn this into a grassy pasture for our cattle or an annual crop field. Through herbicides, intensive grazing and planting other crops, the humans change this land system to whatever it is they want.

Later on, they decide that this is taking too much time & energy to maintain this human-centric ecosystem, so they decide to stop interfering. They expect the wildflowers to come back, but what actually happens is that brambles, bracken and grasses take over. The field is now just a thicket of brambles and is completely unusable. It takes even more energy now to cut back these brambles.

In order to return it to a wildflower meadow, we need intensive human management. We need to cut back all the grasses & brambles (even if we didn't let them grow). We need to 'scratch' the top layer of the soil as chickens or cattle would have done at intervals before humans for the seeds to germinate in. We need to sow a diverse seed mix of some "boom & bust" annual species to keep out grasses & weeds while the longer perennials take root and flower in their second year. We need to regularly cut back growth - the antifragile wildflowers increase their growth with each cut, while the fragile brambles don't like being cut back. Only after 4 years or so of work will the wildflower system be established enough to continue without further intensive human management.

The former is not rewilding, it is abandonment. Rewilding takes energy, resources & time. So too is austerity not "social rewilding" but abandonment. Asset-Based Community Development, the "With" and "By" roads we'll discuss later, is how you re-wild communities.

So the net result is that austerity doesn't actually reduce demand for energy input, it increases it. Not only has it had a devastating effect on our society, but it has also moved demand onto other institutions (e.g. mental health, urgent GP, maternity & social services onto 999 services) and into unpaid professional time - a burden that has been particularly taken on by women - as well as meaning pay cuts for professionals, increasingly out of date infrastructure and technology. Finally, it decreases the quality of care and burns out professionals.

Professional burnout

It is not just the people who are receiving help who are hurt by the "To/For" road, but the people doing the helping too. Spiralling demand means the professional's caseload becomes unmanageable. They are asked to do more and more things they couldn't possibly achieve in an attempt to replace community functions. The financial burden resulting from spiralling demand means resources are cut where it's easiest - from the professional's pay packet. The professional - genuinely well-intentioned - will often work unpaid overtime on top of this to see that people don't go without. In voluntary scenarios, volunteers work all hours for the same reason. All the while, they have to navigate the red tape and the barriers placed in their way, and the frustration this causes, as well as work under the suspicious eye of various regulatory systems, under constant threat of financial or disciplinary regulatory penalty.

Professional morale

On top of the factors mentioned above that will subtract from a professional's morale - worse pay, moral injury, unpaid overtime, suspicion from regulators etc. - there are also factors in institutionalism that fail to create positive morale.

The professionals I've met, on the whole, generally want to care & help, but many of them feel a hollowness, a loss of purpose. Some of them feel like they don't really help that much (solving the wrong problem), that they're meeting their bosses', not their patients' priorities ("To"), that their help isn't appreciated (resistance) and worst of all, that they are just a bum on a seat, a number. This feeling strips them of any sense of purpose. Generally, this is put down to a poor "culture" inside an institution, yet despite drives for institutions to "value their staff", the results have yet to appear.

However, it is not just the gifts & uniqueness of the people they try to help that are lost in the process of institutional care, but also the gifts & uniqueness of the people that are helping. As John McKnight explains in "The Abundant Community", the process of "institutionalisation" is really "depersonalisation". In an attempt to create predictable, managed, standard care, institutions cannot but ignore the unique gifts, skills and contributions of their staff. I think it is impossible for it to be otherwise. Professionals can sense this, that they are not known for their unique gifts, and in fact, attempts at personalisation are actively resisted by the institution, and many professionals get frustrated at the institution's inability to allow them to productively use their gifts. This is very much the process of "alienation" that Marx described occurring in other areas of work and is hugely damaging to professional morale. Again, I hope this book can be seen as an attempt to liberate both the helpers & the helped from a damaging system in which we are all harmed, and so that both that can contribute & be known for their uniqueness - what makes them different from others, not what makes them the same (a qualification).

Does the To/For road do any good?

At this point, you're probably asking whether institutions ever do any good? Despite everything, the answer is a resounding yes, they sometimes do good. I certainly hope that if my appendix becomes inflamed, that an expert professional is on hand to diagnose that problem and surgically remove it.

It's all about balance and exposure. We're not taught that there can be any other way in professional training. We're not taught how our mode of helping can cause higher order harms which we need to be mindful of and plan for. We're not told there is any other way. That's what this book is about.

It's important to note that at no point have I said that institutions or professionals always get it wrong. It's not that institutions or outsiders *cannot* pick the right problem from outside, but that insiders are just *better-placed* to pick the most appropriate solution or goal, with the least amount of side effects, in a way no professional ever could.

Similarly, it is not that there is no room for specialism or expertise and this is not an anti-intellectual text. As previously mentioned, the entirety of human society is built on the division of labour between specialists. It's why we don't work as a doctor one day, a lawyer the next and then a builder the following week. This book just encourages specialists to be more prudent judges of when their expertise is required and to be aware of the system in which they're working. More predictable systems lend themselves well to expert intervention. In less predictable systems, we should seek to understand whether the components can do just as well without outside intervention.

Institutions exist for a material reason, which is that they make use of the economy of scale. We need institutions to leverage that economy of scale on our behalf, because there are some things that cannot be done locally, by community, either for lack of specialisation or lack of scale. We need hospitals, and we need doctors & hospitals that specialise. We're not about abolishing institutions, but asking them to keep in their lane, and only cross lanes if they indicate and are invited in (Cormac Russell). This is the principle of subsidiarity - the problem dealt with at the most appropriate scale.

There are also times when we might say that it is ethical to do "To/For" against the will of the person. For example, nobody would argue that we should wait for an unconscious car crash victim to regain consciousness so that they can invite the emergency services to help. We have laws that enshrine our capacity to consent, but that also permit professionals to act without consent in limited cases.

Other cases are more grey areas, for example, around suicide, euthanasia, mental health, and force-feeding. As discussed, these are all extremely difficult subjects, and even if we get a clear cut answer now, the passage of time can change our views on these things. I hope with the extra energy that institutions could have, they could spend it thinking more about these issues, and with the extra power that communities develop, make sure that their collective views are represented and that institutions work in a way that represents democratic will, not institutional efficiency.

Summary

The "To/For" road, evident by its prominence in society, is a powerful force - for better or for worse - thanks to its economy of scale, the concentration of resources and the power of specialisation. What we can see around us however is the effects of too much "To/For" - dependence, breaking down of community, mistrust, spiralling demand and professional burnout among others. Institutions and professionals need to be prudent about when they intervene, remembering that it is a misuse of power to solve a problem that doesn't belong to you (Cormac Russell), aware of the side effects of this mode of helping and including mitigation in their plans. Wherever possible, institutions should make room for "By" road, and help "with" people where they are invited & required.

Chapter 5:
The "Through" Road

The "Through" road is the next most common mode of helping after "To/For". It is defined by:

- The outsider defines the goals but
- The solution uses the insider's resources

In our language, we often call this mode of working "Volunteering" or "Community Engagement". We see this road used a lot in two main situations:

- Where small organisations within a community are funded by institutions (funders, governments or other agencies) to perform the work of institutions.
- In "traditional volunteering" where volunteers work with(in) an institution to help to meet institutional goals, perhaps for a large charity or

in the volunteering wing of an otherwise paid institution.

Often, you'll hear the question asked "How do we engage the community on this issue" or "Why don't they care about this issue?" which are clear signposts of the "Through" road. What differentiates this from the "By" road, where the majority of community work is still carried out informally, is that it is the institution defining the direction.

Examples of this might be:

- A community garden is funded to improve mental health
- A Men's Shed is funded to run employability courses
- A health care professional prescribes a "lifestyle change".
- Public Health bodies try to improve health (as they define it) in a community
- Health care professionals set up peer support groups where, with their supervision, people manipulate eachother's behaviour, instead of the professional 1-to-1

For many people, this is the pinnacle of what a community does, and lots of people call this "community" work. Many books have been published declaring that they celebrate "community" and yet are restricted to discussion of this road. I've read the writings of many "experts in health & communities" or "consultants in communities" or even organisations who supposedly practice "ABCD", but what they're actually talking about is this "Through" road.

And so, in the same way that helpers are directed down the "To/For" road by its prominence in literature and education, the allure of an income and because the other roads are hidden from view, so too are other people now luring helpers down a new road (and promoting their own personal objectives or causes in the process) who are disillusioned with the "To/For" road and want to do something different & better for the people they're helping. And for the same reasons that people get stuck on the "To/For" road even though they feel it is failing (e.g. the need for a steady wage), helpers get stuck on the "Through" road too. I hope this book will illuminate all the roads equally, helping people to be conscious of the siren call of the "Through" road and choose what road they feel best.

So my warning to anyone venturing out seeking literature on community alternatives is that it is this road you'll read about most often, and the existence of the "By" road will be entirely missed. Red flags are the word "health" (meaning institutionally defined health) or talk about community work in relation to money, funding, government agencies or other institutions.

The qualities that arise from this mode of helping are:

1st Order - Task Level

- The Wrong Problem & Side Effects

2nd Order - Person-level

- The internalisation of negative self-image & dependence

3rd Order - Community-level

- Distortion of community spaces
- Turns community spaces into fixing spaces, not bumping spaces
- Drives unsustainability
- Grows community spaces faster than the speed of trust
- Eventually, it grows community organisations doing "By" into institutions doing "To/For".

4th Order - Cultural-level

- Inhibition through credentialing
- Setting up a two-tier system of volunteering

5th Order - Institutional-level

- Undermining professional workers
- Volunteer burnout

1st Order - Task-Level

The Wrong Problem & Side Effects

These issues have been discussed at length in previous chapters, and they remain a quality of the "Through" road. Just because the community is now doing the leg work doesn't mean that the goals they're pursuing are now automatically correct, because they're still being shepherded by an outsider.

But citizens aren't stupid. Only a small portion of the population engage in this way, made up of the small section of the population for whom their interests and the interests of an institution align, those who wish to gain from the personal benefits of aligning with institutional priorities by volunteering in this way (for example, through the Duke of Edinburgh Award or to launch a future political campaign), and those who have been conditioned to know no other way. We know this because institutions are constantly asking the question: "how do we recruit more citizens for X initiative?". Institutions pay for marketing and behaviour change consultants to help them recruit more. On an individual level, some professionals develop an unhealthy obsession with manipulating people they're trying to help under the guise of "health promotion" or "community engagement".

This also drives the idea that the community is split between "good, active, people who volunteer in the community" and "bad, lazy, people who don't care enough to volunteer". This confusion of moral values with whether you spend your life helping institutions meet their goals, rather than (less visibly) helping your neighbours to meet theirs, is another way of recruiting more volunteers. This moralising in community space, which exists on the "By" road too, is one of the principal dangers for anyone promoting community alternatives, which we'll discuss again later.

On an individual level, in the health sphere, this same process manifests as healthism, which is the biocitizen philosophy that our life is about meeting institutional definitions of health and reducing our burden on the NHS, and the very real discrimination against people deemed to be "unhealthy", such as fat people. Healthism and institutional definitions of health seep into every corner of our culture and throughout community life, and therefore, this is such an important topic that a whole chapter will be dedicated to this later.

In addition, outside the pure health sphere, we see something akin to healthism manifesting, where a good citizen is one who is not a "burden" on institutions and "welfare".

Ultimately, the problem is not that only a small number of people care, but that people in general unconsciously & intuitively understand that the goals pursued aren't relevant to them, and the institutions have got the goal wrong.

2nd Order - Person-Level

<u>The internalisation of negative self-image & dependence</u>

On the "Through" road, the replacement of the professional with a neighbour who acts under their direction still reinforces all the same things as covered in the "To/For" road. The neighbour has generally received some institutional training & credentialing and still defers to institutional goals. The institution is still what stands behind either the professional or the neighbour in this context, only the face has changed.

Despite the community doing the legwork, the "Through" road still reinforces the idea that things will only get better when people from outside come and at least tell us what we need to do and/or fund us to do it. This is reinforced by, and in turn, reinforces, the institutionalisation of the "To/For" road.

The result of this institutionalisation is that we now see, in the community, neighbours acting like institutions: Instead of talking to the neighbours in their street, people straight away set up Community Interest Companies or Charities and apply for funding to pay to fix their neighbours. If funding falls through, then sometimes they go home disappointed that the world doesn't care about their issue as much as it should, and the energy is lost. Sometimes they'll protest or create a petition to put pressure on the institution to give them funding instead.

All in all, the net result of this process is that inordinate amounts of community energy are lost to trying to understand legal structures, writing policies & procedures, writing funding applications (and evaluations if successful), picking themselves up when they aren't successful, and fighting for their issue to be recognised by an institution. If this energy had been directed at meeting their neighbours, connecting their friends and working on the issue in the "informal" space, a huge amount more could have been achieved.

There is some overlap with the "With" road here. After all, isn't funding an institutional resource going to community people who have decided their own objectives? This is true. However, the reason it's included here is that the way that, generally speaking, funding is given out is itself a process that selects for those that align with institutional goals. In this way, it puts institutions in the lead, directing the work, predominantly using the community's "labour" resource, even if funded.

3rd Order - Community-level

Distortion of community spaces

As just mentioned, the way that funding is given out by institutions creates a process that only selects for those that align with institutional goals. This is easy enough to demonstrate: there are no funds available to promote fatness or to give people free cannabis, despite the fact that these things could, in some circumstances, improve the quality of some people's lives.

This means that those community organisations that grow & replicate are ones that promote institutional goals and abide by its rules (e.g. not calling out the government or institutional space *too* effectively), while those that don't align or don't abide by the rules are unable to get access to funds.

This unequal playing field distorts community life away from what really matters to that community to what matters to the institution. Considering the "Wrong Problem" and "Side Effects" again, we can see how this can create direct harm, as well as displacing efforts to do things that would really make a difference in that community. It also confers pseudo-success onto projects that pursue institutional goals, work with formal structures, get funding etc. further contributing to the institutionalisation of community space.

Turns bumping spaces into fixing spaces

One of the most harmful effects of the "Through" road is that it turns spaces that exist in a community as "Bumping Spaces" into "Fixing Spaces".

Bumping Spaces are spaces where real community connection happens, where people show up authentically and naturally form connections. Bumping spaces can be community gardens, a park bench, a party or event, a well designed common area between buildings or so many more things. One of the drivers of our loss of community connection is the loss of these bumping spaces from our town planning & architecture - deliberately promoting "privacy" (isolation) over "connection". Sometimes these bumping spaces naturally draw in people with similar interests (gardening club) or gifts (a choir), others are more diverse (a park bench). These bumping spaces not only give us an opportunity to connect with our neighbours, but with the places where we live. The "placelessness" that is observed is a result of the loss of these bumping spaces.

The "Through" road is responsible for the further colonisation of these bumping spaces by turning bumping spaces into fixing spaces. A fixing space is where someone who has been (or is about to be) given a label comes to get fixed. Sometimes these spaces are newly created (e.g. an Alcoholics Anonymous meeting) and others are converted (a community garden that starts taking referrals for people with mental health labels).

These fixing spaces draw in people who share the same label (e.g. fellow "alcoholics") or those with other labels. Peer support is clearly an important element for some people who want to change their lives and should be available for anyone who wants it. However, the side effects of being surrounded *exclusively* by connections where you are only known by your problems should not be ignored, and this is why we need a balance between peer support and real community. If we remove bumping spaces and turn them into fixing spaces, we deny people the opportunity to find the right balance in their lives.

Funding drives this transformation of bumping spaces into fixing spaces by demanding data & results. Whenever we measure, we're measuring with a purpose, towards an outcome. That outcome is decided by somebody, and if that somebody is a funder, then this is another way in which an outsider directs community life. This comes with all the problems we've already discussed relating to this.

So let's consider an example. Funders come along to a community garden - where, currently, people just show up authentically, share what they feel like sharing and connect with people of a diverse background. The funders see the success of this group and see an opportunity to turn this garden into "Green Therapy" for people labelled with mental health problems.

The deal is struck: the garden gets a paid employee, paid for by the funders, as well as costs covered and a bit of money for other infrastructure projects that'll benefit the labelled group and everyone else too. In return, people just need to fill in a survey about their mental health on joining, and then a few times a year after that.

The garden gets an influx of new volunteers who have been labelled with "mental health" and told by their GP or their social prescriber to turn up to a garden where they'll get their problem fixed. Straight away, the relationship is no longer adult-adult or citizen-citizen, but parent-child, helper-helped, "philanthropist"-"needy" or, more problematically, even seen as a business-customer relationship.

Even though sessions might be integrated (not always in reality, which is even worse), those labelled people turn up with the fixing expectation, and it's not hard to figure out (i.e. new faces) who has come to be "fixed" anyway. There develops two groups - the philanthropist volunteers, giving away their time and energy out of altruism and supposedly receiving little to nothing in return - and the needy consumers, who have come to be fixed.

The need to report data can also start to drive the agenda (the tail wagging the dog). Instead of decision-makers intuitively feeling the system in which they work and listening to the democratic will of the people who work in it, decisions begin to be taken by those "who know things" about mental health to ensure that the data is positive (or more positive). After all, if the data isn't positive enough, the funding might not be renewed, and now their livelihood is at stake. Furthermore, they've used the money to build infrastructure that now entails a liability (all infrastructure does).

Just one pot of funding, just one survey, is unlikely to be sufficient to make the changes that are going on noticeable. In fact, the organisation is likely to see some initial positive growth with these extra resources, reinforcing their decision. Positively reinforced by this, and with the threat of losing the funding they are now reliant on, more funding is sought. This process continues until a critical phase is reached.

This critical phase ends in one of two outcomes. In a few cases, they go on to grow into institutions but for most projects, they simply collapse.

By building in fragility (liabilities), they are no longer able to take advantage of the energy flows around them, but are damaged by it. It often doesn't take long for a sufficiently large stressor to arrive that overwhelms the project's "resilience" and causes it to collapse. That stressor may not even be external but internal, where volunteers no longer turn up because the feel of the space has changed. The "bumping space" that once was there, which created its initial success and drew people there in the first place, no longer exists. It is now an artificial space where they have no stake in its running (possibly only consulted), where people come to get fixed (which most people resist), and volunteers feel that the atmosphere has changed. The organisation loses its support and collapses.

I've watched many organisations go through this process, and they can't figure out what went wrong and go on to repeat the same mistakes. Furthermore, the landscape is littered with the physical and human debris of past projects that have collapsed suddenly - from the jobs lost and reputations tarnished, to the land overgrown and the people made dependent and then abandoned.

As mentioned though, in a small number of cases - for what exact reason has yet to be discerned (but it certainly isn't good leadership) - the organisation muddles through this critical phase and goes on to become an institution, becoming "outsiders" to other communities and even their own. They are still vulnerable to the same threats as just described but usually can survive the most common stressors in the environment.

When people in the ABCD field use the phrase "focus on what's strong, not what's wrong", it's a nice rule of thumb to turn us away from this direction. If we don't focus on what's wrong, we cannot go down this road. Indeed, much of what ABCD celebrates is bumping spaces, and when we train people to "do ABCD", it's largely about stopping turning bumping spaces into fixing spaces, and creating more bumping spaces.

Unsustainability

Cormac Russell will often say that organisations can only grow at the speed of trust. In permaculture design, we also have the design principle "small & slow solutions". This, however, is the very opposite of what happens when those in the community driving seat turn on the institutional Sat Nav. It tells them to put their foot down. On the other hand, when growing using the resources from within a system, it is only possible to grow at a sustainable, natural pace for that system. It is when we begin to import resources from outside our system that we have the capacity to grow faster than a sustainable pace. Our maintenance and further growth is then dependent on the continued flow of resources from outside the system; a very precarious situation to be in.

Furthermore, funders & institutions demand results, and fast. There is an institutionally imposed time frame, with no reference to the many years of investment with little to no return ("results") that organic growth would take.

This also drives growth faster than the speed of trust and forces the use of outside resources.

As an analogy, imagine two gardeners who want to create community gardens. Both have been donated a field to use by the town. One starts slowly, growing a few crops in one corner, using only resources that are found on site or local waste. Materials from the site are composted and used for the soil. Seeds are saved. Labour is only what can be managed from those within the system. Each year, they sell a small bit of their surplus and they use that to add another growing bed. There is no pressure, and so it attracts a steady trickle of core volunteers, who feel they really take ownership over the site. It functions as a bumping space, not a place to do extra work.

It takes many years, but eventually, they stop short of using the whole field. They've realised that certain areas are not suitable for crops and so have put a social area there instead. They also recognise the limits of the resources of the system. When they get to this point, the ecosystem has developed to be able to support the site, and they are confident that it can be left to largely manage itself, and any work still required can be confidently managed in the otherwise busy lives of those within the system. Not only this, but through the building of the system, they have developed a strong relationship with the soil, the land and each other, and they've learnt a huge amount.

The other has been given a field and some funding. So, the money has been used to pay professional gardeners & landscapers to turn the whole field into a large community garden straight away. Some volunteers hear about the project and come and help out for free too. The whole field gets converted and planted up, creating a huge workload right away. To get enough compost for all of this, they have to buy it in. To supplement this, they need to use chemical fertilizers.

The funders want this Community Supported Agriculture scheme they have funded to feed 10 families immediately, so the pressure is on. Volunteers do keep showing up, but they don't feel the same ownership or connection to the project, especially as all decisions are taken by the now paid staff members and "trustees" (mainly in the interests of the funders).

The paid staff member is under so much pressure - having just bought a house and with a new family - that they have frequent episodes of sickness. The paid staff member actually spends more time writing funding applications to secure the future of the site than actually doing the gardening they love. Regularly, volunteers don't quite supply the amount of labour required to manage the site. Some areas have become overgrown, some crops lost. Occasionally they get temporary reprieves when a new "educational course" is started, but they discover this doesn't last long.

There are unforeseen peculiarities with the land - for example, the way a hill shades out a particular corner - that it's now too expensive to fix. Further funding is obtained for "marketing" to get more volunteers on board. The trustees are frustrated that their community just doesn't care about their project. The infrastructure of the site entails a liability - grassy walkways need weeding, the edges need strimming and the wooden beds need repair for rotting. The site needs to bring in professional gardeners from time to time to sort this out. Furthermore, they had the funding to buy a building for socialising but they put it in the windiest spot where they need to pay huge bills to keep it comfortable and causes the building to also need regular upkeep.

All of these processes create more and more dependencies on outside resources - people, money and materials - which piles even more pressure on the organisation to secure *even more* outside resources. Essentially, borrowing from Peter to pay Paul. The system is not resilient, and certainly not antifragile. It is fragile.

One year, the funding application isn't successful. The funders have another shiny new project to fund. The garden goes bankrupt under the weight of its dependencies. The site is abandoned, with no energy remaining to rewild. The volunteers who have been coming to the site to get "fixed" have lost their access totally, despite the fact they could keep one small patch going under their own steam. The paid staff member, already burnt out, now has a reputation as a "bad manager" and struggles to find a new job. They have a breakdown due to the threat of the foreclosure of his new family home. Everyone just mutters how unfair it is that funders have done this. They haven't looked at how this is just the natural conclusion of a *fragile site design* and the dependencies and unsustainability that it created. Meanwhile, the other site might still not have reached its final destination yet, but it has been organic, natural growth, not a boom-bust cycle.

This land-based analogy is a good demonstration, but this occurs even in projects that have nothing to do with land. One must only go out into your community, investigate old bits of land and building, and ask people for their stories, to see its legacy.

Funding as chemical fertilizer

To take the analogy further, we can understand that funding is just like the chemicals that we use in agriculture.

The farmer will select a chemical based on their priorities and their perception of the problem - usually data-driven. Perhaps they think the soil needs more phosphorus, or perhaps the problem is pests. So the farmer uses chemical fertilizer or pesticide on the field and is usually satisfied to see an initial bumper yield. If the intervention doesn't work, it usually is assumed that it didn't work because either not enough chemicals were used (use more next time) or because they got the problem wrong (so try a different one next time). The question of whether it was ever right for the farmer to intervene in the natural system in this way doesn't come up.

Encouraged by the first and subsequent years' increased yields, the farmer is convinced that chemicals are the way to go. However, in the following years, the system obviously breaks down more and more. The yields decrease, forcing the farmer to use even more chemicals. Downstream, the accumulation of more and more chemicals is having unknown side effects on the total ecosystem. What the farmer doesn't understand is that they've actually destroyed the carrying capacity of the soil with chemicals.

Thankfully, society has begun to understand that the use of chemicals is counterproductive in the long term. But the same cannot be said of funding.

Funders, like the farmer, approach the social ecosystem with their own, limited understanding of it. They diagnose a problem based on that limited understanding and primarily through measurements and data, and use their money to solve it, like the chemicals. They are very encouraged by the initial "bumper yield" when the money first begins to flow in. However, they are unaware of the side effects of this money going in which is damaging the ecosystem, and very soon, the carrying capacity of the community degrades. Rather than question whether they might be at all part of the problem, they pour more and more funding into a community, but just do more and more damage. Eventually, they usually give up and attach a label like "uncooperative" or "helpless" to a community, leaving a space for another funder to fill the gap, or the community begins to resist and throws them out.

4th Order - Cultural-Level

<u>A two-tier system of volunteering</u>

Within society, we have a culture of celebrating those who do a certain kind of volunteering - on the "Through" road - far more than we celebrate those who take the "By" road. Some of these "Through" volunteers get awards, honours and reputation. They often go on to get jobs in institutions. To some extent, jobs in institutions *require* some "Through" road helping. For example, if applying to medical school, it would be far more advantageous to have volunteered for a big charity than having done small things for your neighbours, even if you'd learnt and helped more in the latter than the former. In fact, I'd go so far as saying that I'd rather have a doctor who is a good neighbour than one who has done lots of volunteering for charities, but we select for the very opposite.

This has the effect of further institutionalisation of community space, drawing people with energy towards these "recognised" ways of helping and what matters to institutions and away from what matters to them & their neighbours.

Inhibition by credentialing (abiding by institutions rules)

In order to get funding or to volunteer, you need to abide by certain rules, driven by risk aversion & accountability processes that we discussed in the previous chapter, and these rules can consume energy and stop community members from helping.

Small organisations must form into a particular legal structure - usually a social enterprise or a charity (or the legal structure appropriate to your locality). This usually means auditing and the like, which requires a huge amount of work. They also must develop policies & procedures at the institution's request.

Volunteers on the other hand need to hand over their data to be able to turn up. They have to get criminal record & safeguarding checks and need to be trained & credentialed at certain tasks to be able to perform them.

All of this takes energy and may be a level of structure that is inappropriate to the task. Formalisation & structure is okay when that's been driven by internal drivers, as this ensures that the level of formality is correct for the context. However, when this is driven from the outside - for example, by the requirements of funding - it often ends in an unsustainable, inappropriate and ultimately inefficient and damaging amount of structure.

Furthermore, if this is our only way of responding as a community in a crisis, this can be devastating. Contemporary examples are that thousands of people signed up to be "NHS Volunteers" in the COVID-19 Pandemic, but months later, barely anyone had heard a thing. Meanwhile, their energy had dissipated waiting to be "activated" by their app, leaving their communities & neighbours the poorer for it. Similarly, the vaccine rollout in the UK got off to a slow start because so many hurdles were placed in the way of volunteers, taking months to overcome.

5th Order - Institutional-Level

Volunteer burnout

It is not just professionals who burn out, but also the volunteers the institutional functions have been outsourced to. Having to earn money as well as feeling like they have to volunteer to meet the needs in the community puts volunteers in a particularly time-poor and vulnerable situation. During my time in Lesbos, I saw how anyone who had been there for any significant length of time was totally burnt out. They felt the call of duty to care so strongly they were unable to say no to the huge amount of "need" around them, but few recognised that this "need" for outsiders to solve the problem was being created, perpetuated and further grown by the response by NGOs itself. The only way to meet that need was not for more volunteers or for individual volunteers to do more, but to work in a way that actually reduces the need overall ("With/By"). Ram Dass calls this the "Helper's Prison", where helping in this way actually just increases the total amount of suffering overall because the suffering of the helpee is barely relieved but the helper is now also suffering.

Volunteer exploitation & undermining professional workers

We've mainly been considering the most common instance on this road - community organisations paid to do institutional work - but there is also another type - the volunteer wing of various institutions where professionals would have otherwise been paid.

In the UK, this space has grown in recent years as a response to austerity, and the community taking over these "Through" functions has even been celebrated. But what it really means is institutions exploiting the goodwill of volunteers to undermine paid professional work and reduce the budget. Nobody wins in this situation, except the institution themselves.

The volunteer is doing work that would previously have been paid, and if it were still, might have been a post they could have been trained and applied for.

The paid worker has been laid off - or not recruited in the first place - because there are now volunteers willing to replace them.

The recipient of help often receives an inferior level of help to what might have been possible otherwise.

The two examples I'm most familiar with is the introduction of "Community First Responders" and volunteer vaccinators during COVID-19, and so I will use these as an example.

Community First Responders are local members of a community, usually rural, who have undergone some basic training and volunteer to respond to serious 999 instances in order to get there faster than the ambulance. In most instances, the volunteers themselves have to fundraise to purchase the training, the equipment and the vehicle they use. On the face of this, it seems like a really nice initiative - and it would be if this was an optional extra, a nice to have, to supplement the same level of ambulance provision as otherwise.

However, what has actually happened is that ambulance provision has been steadily centralising in urban areas, a move that has been facilitated by Community First Responder schemes, leaving rural areas <u>to have to fundraise for their own emergency care</u> - the emergency care they pay for in the same way as everyone else in the country, except here, they have to pay twice, or face worse health outcomes due to prolonged ambulance times.

Ambulance Services across the country are exploiting these volunteers' time & resources to reduce their budget. If ambulance services covered these areas equally to urban centres, far more ambulances and paramedics would be needed. These first responders could have been trained to fill these posts and more paid work would have been available for paramedics & allied ambulance staff. Furthermore, these rural communities are receiving inferior emergency care as a result. This is unethical in the highest order and is a critical problem to "volunteer" wings of institutions in which otherwise would work paid professionals.

Another example is that while I worked as a vaccinator during COVID-19, I was being paid as a healthcare professional, but some of those I was working alongside, doing the same job as those paid, were working for free. This could have been a paid post for the person or another person if this were not the case. If this is not exploitation, I don't know what is. The only people who benefited from this situation was the institution itself. If this was a business, it would be condemned, but because it's an institution, they get a free pass.

Where do we accept the "Through" road as the most appropriate road though?

Law, governance, ethics, and morality are, in their own way, an enforcement of external priorities and limits on an insider, if their homeostatic direction contravenes this (though thankfully rare). Without diving into a treatise on the pros & cons of law or ethics, we must recognise that many of us, when we try to help, will not want to cross these boundaries. I am not promoting helping someone to break the law or contravene ethical boundaries just because someone wants to, just that we must recognise when we do place those limits on someone, that we are working on the "Through" road and to plan accordingly: how can we minimise the side effects, how can we maximise other choices etc.

Chapter 6:
The "By" Road

When it comes to people consciously going out into the world to help, the "To/For" road is by far the most common, followed by "Through". This is because people who feel their life mission is to help others will either train as professionals or be recruited by institutions as volunteers.

However, the "By" road is *actually* the most common *in general*. This is because the "By" road is filled with people who are not *consciously* going out of their way to help people, but who are just playing the normal roles of citizens, family members, friends and neighbours. People who don't go to meetings and would turn down any reward or recognition for what they're doing. They wouldn't call themselves helpers or carers. Despite this, they contribute significantly to the lives around them and have a significant impact on their community.

For this reason, the "By" road is paradoxically both the most common and the least visible road. That's not to say there are not those who are conscious helpers in the "By" road, for example, those who run small associations (though again, they're likely to underestimate the value of what they're doing). There are also those that we call "connectors" in the ABCD tradition, who both consciously and unconsciously create the conditions for other people to help unconsciously.

However, this is still the minority. This is because the "By" road is <u>everything else</u> that happens informally in someone's life. On the "To/For" and "With" roads, we see institutions & professionals, outsiders, doing the work. On the "Through" road, we see them directing it. But on the "By" road we see what people & communities do for themselves, and in reality, for most people[7], this is the majority of our life.

From grandparents caring for grandchildren to giving someone a lift to work. From staying with a friend for a week between tenancies to that friend telling you a job has come up where they work. From chatting to someone at the bus stop to a smile at the supermarket

---

[7] Those for whom this is not true are often labelled as "institutionalised"

cashier. From meeting up with friends at the pub, to getting together for a meeting with neighbours about litter.

These unconscious everyday actions that we barely consider to be helping (at least to the same degree as professional help) are the actual actions that keep our lives going, that knits our lives together, that create the qualities of community like "welcoming" or "safe". This is the real work. Imagine a world in which these little, seemingly insignificant interactions stopped happening? Nothing would get done. In fact, we got a small taste of this in the COVID-19 lockdowns. But despite the pandemic, communities found new ways to keep "By" life ticking along. One thing is for sure, life would be truly miserable without these things.

But we don't try to measure these actions, and indeed, it is probably best left that way. They are probably immeasurable anyway. They occur entirely in the gift economy - that is, the economy where things are given & taken with no definite return (perhaps only as far as "good karma") - no money changes hands and no contracts are drawn up. Yet this gift economy, though shrinking from institutional invasion, still dominates our lives. It is how we still organise the economy of our family units, of our friends and of our neighbours.

Therefore the examples of the unconscious "By" road are endless. However, beyond the unconscious, examples might be:

- Neighbours getting together to act on something they care about
- People on a street sharing food waste with a neighbour who wants to compost
- Any number of small associations, from book clubs to choirs

Remember that the nature of this road is:
- The problem is defined by the insider
- The resources used is those of the insider

Therefore, it must be remembered, that while citizens can do "by" within their own community for problems that affect them, on an individual level, only the individual themselves can do "by". In this instance, someone who desires to help can only create the conditions for "By" by stepping back and providing the space or serving while walking backwards.

The qualities of "By" road are:

<u>1st Order - Task-level</u>

- Better placed to solve the right problem, the problem that matters to the person or community
- Minimised side effects

<u>2nd Order - Person-level</u>

- Igniting Passion, not resistance

- Increased independence
- Internalised positive self-image
- Creation of supportive relationships

3rd Order - Community-level

- Increased interdependence
- Increased community capacity
- Antifragility, resilience & sustainability
- Rapid community response
- Increased power

4th Order - Cultural-level

- Empowered citizens who feel capable of helping

5th Order - Institutional-level

- Reduced service demand
- Better workload balance for professionals

A lot of the above is predictably the opposite of those found in the "To/For" road. As that chapter was particularly long in explanation, this chapter can be shorter, as it is only necessary to restate from the opposite perspective. Furthermore, the qualities of the "By" and the "With" roads are fairly similar and are spread across this chapter and the next, where it is felt most appropriate to discuss.

1st Order - Task Level

<u>Solving the most important problem to the community or person & minimisation of side effects</u>

This was discussed at length from the perspective of the outsider in the "To/For" chapter. From the perspective of the person or community, they are the best placed to define the goal, the problem or the solution. Being inside the system, they are subject to feedback every day from it. Like the regular driver of a car, they know better than anyone what is normal for that system and what isn't. They know how it'll react to different conditions, what turns it can handle and when to go gentle. While a new driver is more likely to crash if they push it hard, they know how it handles. They are also sensitive to subtle changes in the qualities of their communities and are best placed to change course quickly.

They don't rely on measurements, data and annual evaluations, which inform sweeping, high-stake decisions. On the "By" road, people and communities make lots of small, subtle adjustments as they go. They rely on the "feel" of the situation, as perceived by the person or by the whole of the community and collectivised in a democratic way[8]. It becomes an

---

[8] This doesn't necessarily mean voting. Democracy is much wider than the sense in which it tends to be used in the Western culture. Great examples are consensus techniques, the Quaker tradition of the "feel of the meeting" and "voting with your feet".

organic learning process, co-evolving alongside the other elements of their communities.

Just as institutions don't always get it wrong, it also doesn't mean that citizens or communities always get it right. The point is that they are better placed to do so. Even if the problem was the "wrong" problem, instead of it being a violation done by outsiders, it becomes a learning process owned by the person or community who made the decision.

Here it is worth addressing the freedom to solve problems that are important to us. For most of us, in most areas of our life, we do "by" naturally as we have the freedom to solve the problems that are most important to us at any one time. If tired, sleep. If hungry, eat. However, even with these two examples, one can see how the social structure can prevent us from solving our problems. In the formal economy, economic oppression through denial of access to resources for lack of money, and/or the requirement to work in order to gain access to this economy (which, due to various factors, might be impossible or severely restrictive), can prevent us from solving our problems.

In the informal gift economy too, the time constraints of work imposed by the formal economy alongside other factors we have discussed can severely restrict your access to the social wealth, the assets that exist in your community.

Finally, the main topic of this book has been how the formal, organised help imposes limitations on people's abilities to solve the problem themselves. The message of this book to professionals and institutions is how to step back and increase their freedom, and to citizens is how to unpick the cultural assumptions that restrict that freedom.

2nd Order - Personal Level

<u>Passion</u>

Contrary to the general narrative derived purely from experience in the "Through" road - that people are lazy and will do nothing to better themselves if given the choice - we find not only that actually the opposite is true, but also that they only appear lazy when judging people against *our* values and *our* priorities.

If we remove our institutional spectacles, we will see that people are always trying to make their life better, more secure, more comfortable and doing informal things to help their family, friends, neighbours & communities do the same. The easiest example is to look at retirement - after a lifetime of work and with bodies getting older, a time where you no longer have to work for your income, according to the "humans are lazy" theory, you'd expect pensioners to do nothing.

But this is quite the opposite of the reality in any community. Go to any association, charity, voluntary wing or committee and you'll see the majority of people involved are in their later years. They are the backbone of our community. Elderly people learn new languages, look after gardens & footpaths, volunteer to serve tea in hospitals, play new sports and, in general, "manage" whatever community space still exists in an extremely decentralised, informal manner. And this is quite aside from all the non-associational things they do for others, such as looking after grandchildren or going with friends to hospital appointments. This is really what humans do when freed from the bondage of work. They go out into their communities and do things that give them purpose & meaning and help others in a citizen-citizen or neighbour-neighbour way. It is likely that this would be one of the biggest benefits of Universal Basic Income. This undermines the idea of UBI "pilots" or "experiments" because the majority of the benefits are likely to be qualitative and will not show up quantitatively until much later. Furthermore, UBI doesn't solve the problem of institutional overreach in and of itself, and this will also give distorted results.

However, it would also be absolutely no wonder why people who have been deprived of rest & free time for most of their lives would choose to take a period of rest and recovery where they could, be that in a period of unemployment or after retirement. It is unfair, therefore, to condemn these people as lazy spongers. What people are doing is just finding balance and responding to restriction. If we were given the ability to balance our lives better throughout the life course, perhaps these periods would occur less.

The art of creating the conditions for the "By" road is the art of removing these barriers - barriers we've discussed at length in the rest of the book - and nurturing a culture that calls forth kindness in their place.

<u>Increased independence & Internalised positive self-image</u>

When provided the freedom to begin to do things we care about, on our own or alongside our neighbours, we begin to alter the material reality of our existence. Perhaps we learn a new skill or find that a community mechanism exists that can do what we previously thought only a professional and institution could do. We create and surround ourselves with supportive relationships in our community and this creates the material, physical independence.

The changing material independence then changes our psychological understanding of our reality, from one of dependence to independence, and subsequently a change from a negative to a positive self-image.

Furthermore, your primary relationships begin to be premised on your gifts and not your labels or your problems, which is a very powerful thing to be surrounded by. This de-labelled existence is experienced as hugely liberating by many who have spent huge parts of their life carrying a heavy label around on their back, with it defining who they are in the eyes of others.

By increasing the confidence and the self-image of neighbourhoods and the citizens who inhabit them, we see a turn away from the idea that credentialed outsiders must come in to save us, and towards the idea that we can solve our problems ourselves, and if we can't, we can invite in and negotiate as equal partners with institutions.

3rd Order - Community-Level

Increased interdependence/community capacity

Even more potently, the "By" road increases interdependence. The scaling up of the independence and interdependence created at the personal level, as touched on above, creates community interdependence and capacity, as well as the psychological sense and reality that we can depend on each other in a citizen-citizen way. We weave new relationships and connections that we can call upon in the event that we need them.

This increased capacity of the community soil allows citizens to deal with issues that are important for that community, and to grow more associations and more relationships, and a better community. All of this further increases soil capacity, and so on. When we can deal with our problems closer to home, we don't need to turn to institutions or outsiders to solve all our problems, and professionals can be left to concentrate on doing well what they <u>are</u> needed for.

This is a reversal of the displacement of community connections we discussed previously. It is the recreation of the left-hand image, rather than the right hand one. The art of community building is the reweaving of these connections.

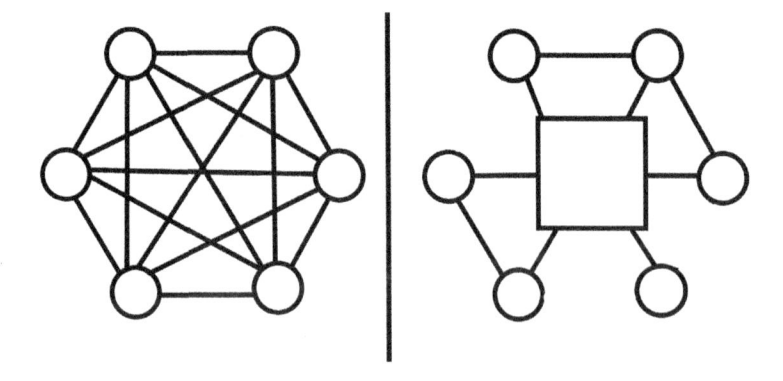

<u>Rapid crisis response</u>

In the event of a crisis, strong local networks can respond much quicker and more effectively. We saw this in the COVID-19 crisis as well as during heatwaves, floods and other crises. Neighbours are able to call upon their relationships and the gift economy to secure resources and achieve things far faster than an institution can mobilise. This ability is enhanced by not having to have meetings and navigate bureaucracy, which institutions, professionals and those taking the "To", "For" and "Through" road are constrained by. The building of an ability to respond rapidly in a crisis is a side-effect of the growth of community capacity and connection.

The proliferation of bumping spaces

Bumping spaces are the gateway into communities and, ultimately, the social wealth. Bumping spaces are anywhere that people in a community can come together and create new relationships and find community. These are critical, especially for people who have been labelled out of community, who have been solely in fixing spaces, and for those newly arriving in a community. Out of these bumping spaces hatch even more associations, ideas and bumping spaces.

Bumping spaces are naturally created when communities do things without institutions and labelling and when spaces are horizontally organised - as citizens helping each other - rather than hierarchical (i.e. paternalistic helping), and are both a symptom and a creator of connected communities. I would argue that the creation and maintenance of bumping spaces is the most important component of building communities.

More sustainability

By allowing communities to grow in an organic way and to conduct their own natural self-healing, communities and their organisations grow more sustainably - for both the community and the ecosystem.

It is almost impossible to overextend yourself and become unsustainable if you derive your energy and resources internally (to your system) and you complete the circle of giving and receiving: no giving without receiving, no receiving without giving. When people and communities come together on this road, it is naturally more sustainable. As previously discussed elsewhere, it is when energy is imported from elsewhere (i.e. institutional funding, professional labour etc.) and projects are driven to institutional timelines, faster than the speed of trust, that sustainability is lost. We'll discuss sustainability more in Chapter 9.

Increased power

We often see power as a zero-sum game. If they have power, I do not, and to get more power, I need to take it from them. This theory doesn't resonate with me.

I see power as our ability to do things, specifically, that which we feel is necessary for our communities, ourselves and our health. As a scaling up of the increased power that we discussed earlier on the "task-level", amplified by the increased connectivity in a community, the more things done "By" a community, the more power it grows.

The zero-sum game idea is derived from looking solely at the formal economy, in which power is measurable through money, and in this instance, it is true. We can only gain economic power at the expense of another. If our capacity to do what we need is only mediated by the formal economy, and the resources are in the hands of others, then this is a justification of our power struggles.

But these are not the only resources available to us. Within our communities, there are huge swathes of resources mediated by the gift economy, including lots of things that grow with more use (unlike money) like gifts, skills, knowledge, love and connection. There is a huge capacity for doing things together with our neighbours that is immediately available to us through communities. We don't need to vote for, beg or fight for the scraps from merciful powers. We can grow our power through our communities. In the gift economy and in communities, power is not a zero-sum game, but a resource that grows more with use. It is the true rising tide that lifts all boats. By giving you more power, I also find more power myself.

Then when a community becomes powerful in this way, through connection, it will be able to go into the formal economy and demand economic power in a significantly more effective and more democratic way than a group of powerless residents begging for power. When a strong, connected, powerful community moves to demand a fairer distribution of power, nothing will be able to stand in its way.

4th Order - Cultural-Level

<u>Unpicking credentialism & empowered helpers</u>

In a community where people have internalised a positive self-image, have a rich network of connections and a sense that they can rely on each other and have a good sense of the resources and assets already within their community's ownership, there comes a culture of empowerment.

When things need to change in the neighbourhood, they don't look to professionals or institutions for expertise or permission, they know they are the experts and need no permission. They don't try to secure outside resources from those same institutions, they begin with the resources they already have. They know they can look to their neighbours, and their neighbours will respond.

Cormac Russell talks about creating communities where not only do random acts of kindness occur, but a community in which exists a culture that actually calls forth kindness. This is what the opposite of credentialism looks like; the positive side of the coin. It is a culture where people are empowered to be kind and to help their neighbours, not one in which they feel they are not qualified or credentialed enough to help, or where they feel it is not their place.

5th Order - Institutional-Level

As there is a lot of overlap, we'll discuss the 5th Order (institutional level) in the next chapter.

Chapter 7:
The "With" Road

The "With" road is where communities work with institutions to reach their goals or to solve problems as they define them, defined as:

- Community defines the goal, the problem or the solution
- The primary resources used are institutional or professional in nature

In other places, we call this mode of helping "partnership", "co-production" or "shared decision making" in the true sense of the word [9].

---

[9] Be wary though because "Through" road initiatives tend to hi-jack these terms.

This road is the last and, in my opinion, the best road that institutions can travel when helping. While lots of institutions & professionals are interested in doing ABCD and are trained in it, it is a misconception to believe that they can actually walk the "By" road (except where the professional is acting in their capacity as a citizen in their own time, of course), which leads to lots of confusion. The institution and professional can serve while walking backwards ("With" road) **to create the space & conditions for those they're helping to walk the "by" road,** but by definition, they cannot actually do it.

Examples of "With" road might be:

- An open funding pot that can be accessed by a group of neighbours who want to do something in their community, regardless of what it is.
- Person-led healthcare, where the professional is on hand to help with a particular issue if invited but doesn't overstep.
- Invited specialist input which is designed to develop the person or community's resources to be able to hand back as quickly as possible.
- Personalised budgets.

The qualities associated with this type of helping are:

1st Order - Task Level

- Solving the most important problem to the community or person
- Minimised side effects

2nd Order - Person Level

- Resolution of problems that cannot be resolved by the community or person alone ,without increasing dependence (i.e. non-dependence)
- Creating the space for the person to walk the "By" road and find independence
- Helping in a horizontal way without need for labels or stigma

3rd Order - Community Level

- Helping without displacing community capacities
- Creating the space for communities to walk the "By" space and find interdependence, etc.

4th Order - Cultural Level

- Increased trust between communities & institutions
- Helping without creating credentialism or displacing power

5th Order - Institutional Level

- More manageable workload for institutions & professionals, improving quality of care
- More sustainability

Creating Space for the "By" Road while doing "With"

It is an easily levelled criticism to say that doing "With" does not *necessarily* create the space for "By", and that is correct. However, doing "With" is an essential prerequisite to that space creation. So the question arises, how might we create that space?

Various strategies have been proposed, forming a core theme of ABCD literature. Personally, I think the critical step is asking some questions at the start of any helping process, and repeatedly ask throughout. Here are some helpful questions I propose asking, though this list isn't definitive.

1. Have I been invited in to help?

This question ensures that you really are on the "With" road and that you're there asking these questions because you've been invited by the person or people that it concerns, not because you've assumed your skills are needed. If so, then:

2. Can the person/people do this for themselves? Is their capacity hidden from themselves?

As we've discussed in other chapters, the psychological and cultural changes as a result of widespread institutionalisation of helping has caused people's gifts and capacities to be hidden even from themselves. "With" practitioners genuinely believe in people's capacities and will seek to discover if they exist first. If the person concerned decides that they still do not have the capacity (not the "With" practitioner), then:

> 3. Is there someone in the community who has the capacity to do this informally, without the institution getting involved?

"With" practitioners will then explore the person's community and network to see if the capacity exists there, but is hidden. Many things can be resolved better informally, without institutional bureaucracy. If successful, it weaves a connection and returns a function to the community, and unlocks all the other benefits of "By". If not, then:

> 4. Can the person or community do this with a little bit of help from the institution?

Does the person or community just need something small from the institution to be returned back to being able to do this in the "By" space. For example, do they just need a small amount of money to get started? Or a little bit of teaching? This question prevents "With" helpers from just diving straight in if no informal capacity is found, and is true "With" help. It causes us to think whether something small will return the community to capacity. If not then:

5. Is there really no alternative from the institution doing this?

There are definitely instances where communities and people cannot achieve something, for example, heart surgery or international redistribution of food from areas of plenty to areas of famine. However, this final question gives us pause, understanding that things are always best done by the person or people, considering whether there is some creative way to avoid the institution taking on the task.

It is in this way that we can create the space for "By" while walking the "With" road. It's important to note that this is not a one-time

1st Order - Task Level

Institutions solving the right problem

Building on the analysis of the right problem in previous chapters, walking the "With" road means supporting the person or the community, even if you think they're wrong. To only help them when you think they're right, when their goals align with your institutional goals, or when what they're doing meets your institutionally defined standard of health is not co-production or partnership, but the "Through" road. It looks like the unconditional empathy I've witnessed in some GP surgeries and other institutions or the bottom-up support provided by the United Voices of the World trade union (in contrast to more traditional unions that do "To", "For" and "Through".).

This commitment to work with people even if you think they're wrong calls for more rounded institutions. Professionals only being available to help with certain problems is "helping only when you think they're right" by proxy. As institutions, it also means to stop looking at "demand" as a problem to be managed and instead signals from competent communities in the lead.

For example, the Choose Well campaign is a UK NHS campaign to convince patients to enter through the right NHS door for their problem. I've written about the problems underpinning this at length elsewhere, but a brief summary here serves to illustrate the different ways to view demand.

One of the central components of the Choose Well campaign is that people should stay away from accident & emergency departments unless their problem is serious. The obvious contradiction that people go to A&E departments precisely to consult a doctor on whether their problem *is* serious or not aside, this campaign, by assuming the population to be selfish, misusing idiots, fails to appreciate that it is its own failure to provide the right doorways into the institution. O'Cathain et al. (2019)[10] shows clearly that one reason people attend A&E in the UK is because they cannot get a timely resolution of their problem elsewhere. What is being "demanded" is a timely face to face consultation with a healthcare professional when needed. But when the doors open to them are 999 for an ambulance, or the A&E department now/today, a phone consultation or the General Practitioner in 2 weeks, it's obvious why someone might go to A&E or call 999. They're not asking for the mobile ICU of an ambulance or the huge technical capacity of the A&E to be brought to bear on their problem, but just a timely face-to-face assessment. By assuming incompetence, they miss the obvious solution and the possibility their patients might actually be right.

Another example is the supposed "misuse" of the ambulance service for mental health issues, which are designated as being more appropriate for specialised mental health services by people behind a desk. Again the assumption is that the person has chosen incompetently and needs educating, berating or otherwise manipulating to ensure they choose the "correct" service (in the eyes of the

---

[10] O' Cathain, A. et al (2019) "'Clinically unnecessary' use of emergency and urgent care: A realist review of patients' decision making" *Health Expectations (23:1) pp19-40. Doi:10.111/hex.12995*

institution/professional - and we've already discussed how limited their knowledge of the situation can be).

If we are instead open to the idea of helping even when we think someone is wrong, or open to the idea they may even be right even if we think they're wrong, then we see the problem differently. One need only compare the difference in care to understand supposed misuse. The reputation amongst users of mental health services of those same services is pretty poor all-around. Often, all that someone wants is someone to talk to, perhaps to help them in some small way. Normally what they get, however, is a phone consultation and are told they are "safe" and so no professional intervention is needed and to speak to their "key worker" in a few days. This isn't the fault of those professionals necessarily, as they have to prioritise the most urgent cases, made worse by the increasing demand as a result of everything we've spoken about. The fact that someone needs to call a mental health service for someone to talk to is also indicative of the ways we have lost community capacity to fulfil that function. Absent this, examine the current alternative: if they call 999, then two people will come to see them in their home pretty quickly and (have at least no other choice but to) spend a bit of time listening to their problems, and perhaps take them to A&E or call the mental health services back, so, even if this ultimately leads nowhere, it at least feels like someone cares and they are being taken seriously, as competent, valid people.

Rather than berating people for using the ambulance service for mental health issues, we should first look at why they have to use an institution in the first place and help return them and their communities to being able to deal with this issue, and secondly, look at what factors lead a competent, informed, morally sufficient person to make certain decisions. The answer then becomes obvious.

Ultimately, helping on the "With" road works on different assumptions to the "To/For" road:

- Institutions and professionals should help only when invited in
- Institutions and professionals should help even if they think someone is wrong, being open to the idea that it might be the person who is right and the professional wrong
- Helping non-judgmentally, and with no pressure from the institution or professional
- Just because someone asks for help doesn't mean they are incompetent and the basic assumption is that people act rationally and competently.
- Demand for services are signals from competent rational users, not something to be managed with marketing, manipulation and beration
- There should be no wrong door into institutions.

2nd Order - Person-Level

<u>Resolution of problems that cannot be resolved by the community or person alone without increasing dependence (i.e. non-dependence)</u>

Sometimes problems do need institutional resources to be solved. If a person or community is asking for help and an institution refuses to help because of this book, for fear of causing dependence, they have entirely misunderstood. This is negligence and abandonment. There is a qualitative difference between being invited in and not.

However, there does remain some possibility of dependence, so those walking the "With" road should always work in such a way as to return the person and/or their community to have the capacity to deal with the problem as soon as possible. We posed some questions earlier in the chapter that should help you to do this.

Working in this way involves, firstly, trusting that the person or community can actually take over these functions from you. From there, it's about creating the conditions for those walking the "By" road to take back over. For some things, this is as simple as not overreaching in the first place, and perhaps imparting some knowledge. For someone who has been heavily institutionalised, however, then it's about skillfully educating, gradually handing back functions, reweaving community connections and increasing confidence, all with the person or community in the lead.

I don't pretend that this is easy. There is a practised art; the art of serving while walking backwards. I am not the one to write the book on exactly how to do this, as there are people far more experienced in this than I am. I'm sure there are bound to be skilled reconnectors who could write this book in the ranks of link workers, progressive GPs, support brokers, Acceptance & Commitment Therapists or intuitive eating nutritionists, amongst others.

This is the road that *should* be practised by link workers (a.k.a. social prescribing) or community animators: working to undo the damage done so far by the "To/For" road. Rewilding communities. Unfortunately, though link workers first appeared organically on the "With" and "By" roads (according to their particular form), since being scaled up and rolled out by the NHS, they appear to be predominantly on the "Through" road. More on this later.

Note however that this road, done right, is more about *not creating* dependence rather than creating independence (thus, non-dependence). Though professionals and institutions *can*, in the aforementioned roles, promote independence, this is only by creating the conditions in which "By" care can flourish, which is the only way of creating independence. Functions will naturally be reabsorbed by a community when the "By" road is strong.

3rd Order - Community Level

<u>Helping without displacing community capacities</u>

Helping on the "With" road ensures that community capacities are not displaced when an institution or professional helps because, if the questions at the start are asked correctly, it cannot be displaced because it doesn't exist to begin with! However, if appropriate, all efforts should be made to re-create the capacity and return the function to the "By" road.

This is reminiscent of Robert S Mendelsohn's (a paediatrician) question when presented with a poorly child: "what would your grandmother do?" By asking this question, Mendelsohn avoided displacing community knowledge with his own professional knowledge.

4th Order - Cultural Level

<u>Increased trust between communities & institutions</u>

Working in a "With" way eliminates the possibility of corruption or exploitation ("To" road). If the community or the person is truly the one setting the goals, the one in the lead, then the institution cannot secretly benefit (or they can only do so as an unexpected pleasant side effect).

Working in this way would begin to reverse some of the mistrust and heal the broken relationships between some communities. Experiencing that they can approach an institution without judgement, without fear that they'll take over and impose their agenda, will go some way towards this.

I would also hope that with more trust, we'd see more understanding and humanity when it comes to harmful accidents in the institutional space, which is bound to happen. Perhaps then we can look at accountability structures anew and look at ways to ensure accountability without bias towards unaccountable events.

5th Order - Institutional Level

<u>More manageable workload for institutions & professionals, improving quality of care</u>

As the capacity of communities and the confidence of their members grows, problems that institutions felt "inappropriate" will become solvable closer to home, by the gift economy of their communities, and less of these problems will arrive at the institution's doorstep. Not through any coercion or development of higher moral reasoning or education, but in a totally organic way as a side-effect of the community building process.

I would also hypothesise that in a strong community, people would need to use institutions less overall as their health & lives improve. For example, not only will some community matters that are currently dealt with by the police be dealt with by a strong competent community, but there would also be less crime, and so even less need for police. Another example might be that, not only are lower-level medical concerns dealt with by the community, but also as the peaks and troughs of people's lives are smoothed by the gift economy of a strong community, there would be less stress and perhaps fewer health crises (e.g. heart attack) overall, and thus less demand at the institutional level again.

In such an environment, institutions and professions can focus on doing an excellent job of the things that they are needed to do, rather than spreading themselves too thin and doing everything poorly. Professionals can have time to care, to work "With" rather than "For", and to be able to plan to enter & exit lives in a sustainable, non-harmful way. Professionals could find space to contribute their real gifts, and find purpose and meaning in their work, as well as balancing their own work-life needs.

By reducing and beginning to create the conditions for reversing institutionalisation, communities, neighbours and people will be empowered to retain more and more functions within the system, with the net result of reducing the burden that falls on institutions and professionals. However, this can't be the driving force of the change, otherwise, it is "To/Through" and it will ultimately undermine itself. If reducing budgets isn't the goal, then this creates even more space for professionals to do more deinstitutionalisation and help in a more considered way. If reducing budgets is the goal, then services will remain just as strained, undermining the ability of institutions and professionals to hold off from more efficient "To/For" help, and therefore reversing the trend.

Limits to "With"

The "With" road is more positive than the "To/For" road, but it is still only a 'least harm' approach. On the "With" road, communities can leverage the economy of scale, expertise and concentration of resources offered by institutions & professionals while remaining in the driver's seat and without degrading community resources.

However, it cannot do lots of the things that only the community, working on the "By" road can do. It cannot increase independence or heal the institutionalised mindset. Institutions, by stepping back, by doing "With" instead of "For", create the conditions in which this can flourish, but they cannot do it themselves.

Furthermore, to reiterate, there may be legal, ethical and moral limits to the "With" road, as addressed at the end of the chapter on "Through".

Part 2: Springboards for Discussion

In Part 1, we've covered the Helper's Crossroads model in depth. However, the model is only looks at the world from one direction, and it leaves many things unanswered. Part 2 is a loose collection of individual essays that are related but not directly about the Helper's Crossroads model. Some address contemporary issues, for example, the role of Social Prescribing, some are too important to leave out of the discussion, for example, the chapter on Health, and others are of simply of interest, such as the Permaculture Principles. Each indicates a new direction we can walk on our investigation, and is intended a springboard to further discussion. Some of these chapters may end up being preludes to further books.

Chapter 8:
The Roles We Play

In the previous part, we explored what different modes of helping look like from the standpoint of the crossroads. You may still be wondering how this might apply to your work or your own neighbourhood. We might all have the same map, but how do we use it? Some of us are driving a car, others a bike and others are on foot. To answer this, we'll look at these crossroads from the perspective of how they're used, introducing a number of roles that appear in the helping spaces that tend to occupy different roads. These roles are organic and loose rather than rigid roles, and each specific will look different, appropriate to the local context in which that person finds themselves. There are some things in common, however, that allow us to group them in this way. I have also probably missed some important roles, so this isn't an exclusive list.

The roles are:

- The unconscious professional
- The prudent professional
- The gapper
- The community animator
- The unconscious citizen
- The community connector

The Unconscious Professional

This is the professional who walks the "To/For" road, often entirely unaware of the map. It is currently the default role in institutions and a role that I have personally played too. The unconscious professional, with entirely good intentions, will often try to reach into community space and solve problems that might be better solved in a different way.

The Prudent Professional

The prudent professional is a professional who, in their own practice, is using the map to inform their decisions and spend the majority of their time on the "With" road. They only turn up when invited, and they are careful to keep the other person in the driver's seat. They are also careful not to fix problems that don't belong to them.

Where people invite them in but want the prudent professional to move to the "To/For" road, they instead practice the skilful art of moving as many functions back to the "By" road as possible. When doing things "with" people, the prudent professional always plans how to not create dependence and how to create the conditions for their help to no longer be required.

Professionals will never be unnecessary. However, the unconscious professional assumes more roles & work than they are needed (or invited) to. Prudent professionals discover their "legitimate residual role" (Credit: Tom Dewar), which is that which remains after they have returned all possible functions and capacities back to communities and citizens.

Almost any professional can be a prudent professional, but some professions where they have really ingrained the art of being prudent are Support Brokers and Intuitive Eating Nutritionists, amongst others.

The Gapper

The Gapper is generally a professional who speaks both the institutional language and the community language, though not necessarily. There is also a reasonable overlap between the role of the prudent professional and the gapper. The difference is that while the prudent professional is focussing on their own practice, the gapper acts on a more outward, institutional level, either as a persuasive peer or as a manager.

The gapper understands the map on an almost instinctual level and is able to discern who is setting the agenda and who is doing the work. Gappers try to create a dome of protection over community spaces to protect them from institutional overreach. They seek to protect the bumping spaces and community capacities that exist in the community.

They are called "gappers" because they help institutions and professionals mind the gap between the institutional and community world. To some extent, I am fulfilling the role of a gapper in writing this book.

By helping an institution to serve while walking backwards, they help relocate resources to the community space from the institutional space. One of the most celebrated "gappers" in the ABCD space is Jerome Miller of "Last One Over the Wall" fame, but many others achieve great things with no recognition.

The Community Animator

A Community Animator is an outsider - usually paid - whose role is to create the conditions for "By" _within_ a community (as opposed to a gapper, who creates the conditions for "By" within an institution). You can think of this role as the "ecological gardener" of the community space. They actively seek to make visible the invisible community assets, to find out people's skills, gifts, to find out what people are passionate about, to create &

nurture bumping spaces and to reweave connections. They are not and should not be essential to the community, but, done in the right way, they can work as a catalyst for ecological regeneration.

In many cases, they are really a subsection of "prudent professional", and so all the same descriptors apply. They ensure that they do not become a point of dependence and they only enter when invited.

The Unconscious Citizen

The unconscious citizen will naturally walk the "By" road in their own lives and in the lives of their neighbours & family. The unconscious citizen is <u>the most important role of all</u> here, as it is the actions of unconscious citizens that create the vast majority of community life, change and help. This fact is pretty unquantifiable because of the invisibility and subtleness of it all, but if we really think about our lives, I think this truth is self-evident.

There is some overlap here between the unconscious citizen & the unconscious "community connector".

The Community Connector

The Community Connector fills much the same role as a Community Animator, except that the Connector belongs to the system in which they work - often unpaid.

Some might have actively chosen to play this role perhaps through exposure to ABCD, but many do so naturally, without ever realising what they're doing, and certainly wouldn't claim any sort of role title or award. They often fill this role by instinct and just out of a desire to be a good neighbour. Where the community animator might be the ecological gardener, the community connector might be the humble bee, pollinating their community and creating the links between different individuals. The community connector compared to the animator, as the bee to the gardener, is far more important and far more critical to their ecosystem.

From an ecosystem perspective, we could understand these community connectors as natural healing agents of a community. When connections in the system have been broken down by external actors, the community begins to heal those connections with "community connectors".

Chapter 9:
Community Permaculture: Principles of Sustainable Organisation Design

When we come together in association with our neighbours, we naturally relate to eachother in some sort of structure (even if that structure is to have no structure). We can call this structure an "organisation". These organisations should be structured and plan according to the internal needs of that organisation and what they're trying to achieve. However, the cultural damage of the "Through" road, however, has created a tendency to mimic institutional designs. I have observed time and time again how this creates liabilities, fragility, burnout and ultimately collapse in all but a very small number of cases (who go on to become institutions themselves). In order to consciously combat this, in this chapter I apply the permaculture principles of sustainable (eco-)system growth to human communities and organisational design to provide a light touch guide for how things can be done differently.

It is a loose guideline because _you_ are the person who knows best about your situation and what the right thing to do is. I hope more than anything to show you just that there is another way and to give you confidence that, where you doubt the well-worn "Through" path, to depart and do what you really feel like doing.

The first thing to remember is that we're trying to influence emergent properties, not mechanical properties, and that we're working with complex adaptive systems, not clockwork. This means we have a lot to learn from Permaculture and other models that deal with complex adaptive systems and that is why I'm using the principles of permaculture design as a basis for these principles of sustainable community organisation design.

The second thing to remember is that the "Through" path will show you the way to rapid organisational growth and high personal profit (at least in the short-term). If that's what you think is needed, I am no one to say otherwise, so go ahead. But, as previously mentioned, be aware that for every one that graduates to being a true institution, the "Through" path leads to many more organisations "going bust", leaving behind a trail of destruction of people's livelihoods and the communities in which they work. I'm more interested in sustainability & antifragility, and so I hope the principles in this chapter help you towards those goals if that is what you seek too.

Thirdly, this guide is primarily for citizens, but there is some applicability to professionals too. It is not a guide on how to "do ABCD" because citizens who choose their own priorities and act on them are already "doing ABCD". The purpose of outlining these principles is to give some guidance on creating sustainability in community design, in opposition to the "general way of doing things" which undermines it, or those that want rapid growth.

Lastly, I will predominantly use the word sustainability as it'll be more familiar to the reader, but we must be clear about what we mean by sustainability. Sustainability is often used interchangeably with resilience, but this is not how I mean sustainable here. Nature is not sustainable because it is resilient, but because it is antifragile (i.e. it grows stronger in response to stress, disorder & chaos). By mimicking nature, these principles aim to help create antifragile designs, not resilient ones. In this way, we create sustainability.

It is worth noting that antifragility is also created as an emergent property of a system in which individual nodes are fragile - the easiest example is evolution, where individuals in a species are fragile to stressors but this creates species-level antifragility i.e. evolution. Therefore, there is a role for fragility in community organisations in making the overall community anti-fragile. While this chapter is going to talk about organisational sustainability, it is worth bearing in mind throughout that what we *really* want is antifragile communities, not immortal organisations, and therefore sometimes organisational structures will need to collapse for community growth to occur. No organisation should be too big or too precious to fail, and these principles, as well as everything else set out in the book, helps ensure this.

1. Observe & Interact

As in the permaculture principles, this comes first because it precedes any active change. Wise farmers will observe their new site for 4 seasons before they make any changes. They observe particularly the rhythm of "vectors" - external sources of energy - that interact with the site, namely, the sun, rain, wind, animals, humans, noise, views etc. They are not just passive observers however, so they interact with the site to learn about it. They go and see what a particular piece of soil looks like in the rain, in the sun, in the snow, they dig a small hole and see what it's like underneath. They develop relationships with the site.

Through this process of observation, a wise gardener will understand the system in such a way as to achieve what they want with **the minimum change to the system for the maximum impact (see 2.)**

For example, an impulsive gardener who acquires a site in spring might know nothing of the river that runs through the middle of their field in the winter rains, putting infrastructure & plants in its path through the summer. They also create expensive & energy-intensive watering solutions for those same plants. But when the winter rains come, the fields & the buildings become flooded, causing crop loss and damage to the buildings. We not only waste energy & money when we have to deal with the consequences of an avoidable mistake like this, it's also energy- & money-intensive to reverse this. The gardener, not wishing to lose the money put into the buildings & fields, embarks on an expensive landscaping project to redirect this river. However, this causes further problems & flooding in other areas of the site, until the force of nature bursts the landscaping and floods the field again.

The wise gardener acquiring the same site will have observed it for a full 4 seasons before making any relatively permanent changes. They saw the river that arose in winter and began to store some of this water in tanks that could be easily gravity fed in summer. The design incorporated this river and used it for its benefits, as opposed to treating it as a problem. They worked with nature, rather than against it.

In a similar way, a wise citizen will observe and interact with the community in which they wish to "design" a solution for an appropriate amount of time (a specific time cannot be prescribed) before they make any new changes. They will get to know their community, what makes it tick, its history. They will meet people on their street and the next street and onwards. They will look under every stone for assets that can be used.

We do this to ensure that we are trying to solve the right problem. We do this to know what it is we already have - the assets of our neighbours - so that we can know what we need - the resources of outsiders, purchased through the market. Normally, we'll find that almost everything can be sourced within our neighbourhood when we begin to see the gifts & resources of those around us, rather than seeing them as problems to be fixed.

We don't always start observation from a blank slate, however. We may have already performed our observation & interaction through the decades we have lived in a community - this is why residents are always naturally much better at understanding what communities need than professionals. However, it is important to note that we might have spent our entire lives only understanding the problems in our community, without taking the time to also understand the assets. We also may find a cumulative written & oral tradition about our community & community building in general which can be used as a foundation for our own observations to build on.

The general purpose of this principle is to take things slow, to exercise caution and to balance against the impulse to do things straight away. There is no set way to do this, but I might suggest:

- Search out the assets that already exist in your community
- Meet and create genuine relationships with people in your community
- Understand what has been tried before - what worked, what didn't?
- ABCD techniques such as Listening Campaigns and doorknocking

2. Use small & slow solutions

Even after a period of observation, we shouldn't begin to think that we now know everything we need to know to make large sweeping changes. This comes second because this is how we should proceed when we start to make changes - we use small & slow solutions, not large & fast ones. **We should aim to achieve the biggest impact with the smallest changes to the system.** Before a period of observation, this would have been impossible, but now that you understand the natural rhythms and what you already have in the community, you will be informed enough to be able to make small changes for large impacts. This is one of the most important aspects of the observation period.

However, we've discussed previously that we never truly know a community system, and we also know that complex adaptive systems can have really large reactions to very small changes. However, this is both something to be cautious about, and a source of inspiration. In the first instance, we must be cautious so we can assess the result, including unintended side effects, of small, gradual changes. However, on the other hand, this also means that we don't need large input to create large changes. With clever design, informed by observation, we can achieve big outcomes in our community with the smallest changes - perhaps even something as small as an introduction of two people.

In the medical world, they call this "titration". Too little of a particular medication has no effect, while too much causes unbearable side effects, and way too much will kill you. Medicine often doesn't know what the exact right dose will be for each person. So, they slowly increase the amount of medication until it achieves the desired effect with the minimum side effects. This is why your family doctor will often start you on a low dose of a medication and increase slowly

We must also "titrate" our changes in communities for the same reason. Many interventions, often driven by funding & institutions, are large & fast - a lethal dose to the unseen community mycelium. Worst of all, the same outcome could have been achieved with a much smaller dose, leaving community capacity intact.

As we can see, the "Through" road creates unsustainability through the exact opposite of these first two principles. When funders & institutions get involved, there is often no time allowed for observation or small & slow solutions. It also gives us the artificial, external energy upfront to overextend ourselves if we're not careful.

So you might remember from Chapter 5 the analogy of the two community gardens and how the principles of observation and small & slow solutions protected one from overextending itself. Just as many enthusiastic gardeners will turn over their whole garden to growing veg in one go and realise later that they don't have the capacity to maintain it all, an enthusiastic social gardener might create a project and realise that they and their neighbours don't have the capacity to maintain it, causing it to collapse in the long run. Small & slow solutions protect against this impulse, creating sustainability and ultimately, room to _enjoy_ the process alongside your neighbours.

So the principle of using small & slow solutions helps us to avoid unintended consequences, enables us to use the properties of complex adaptive systems to our advantage for the least energy (including money, time etc.) input for maximum effect (titration) and helps us ensure that we only take on as much as is sustainable to maintain in the long term, ensuring we grow at the speed of trust.

3. Obtain a yield

The question that might arise from these two principles is: how can we grow in a way that is sustainable? How can we know?

The third principle is to "obtain a yield" - which means that you should aim to derive surplus from the things that you do and the changes you make. This surplus doesn't have to be money necessarily. It might be energy, time, inspiration, knowledge, other physical resources, skills or any other thing you can imagine.

In fact, we shouldn't just aim to simply obtain a single yield from any element of our design, but many in Permaculture suggest that every element in a design should serve at least 3 purposes - if it doesn't, it needs to be changed (perhaps moved to a different location) to do so. This process is very useful in itself as it forces us to consider qualities in a design that aren't often considered (e.g. the enjoyment in a process, the connection between neighbours) and also improves efficiency, enabling us to achieve the greatest impact with the smallest change (one element meeting three functions instead of three meeting one each).

This "yield" - surplus money, energy, time etc. from the small changes you've made - should then be the resources used to grow, not external resources like professional time or funding.

By following this principle - by intentionally creating a surplus early and using it to grow - it is very difficult to overextend, to introduce fragility or to grow faster than the speed of trust.

We only need to look to nature for the results of a slow but sure reinvestment of surplus resources to create sustainability. The rainforest is one of the most vast and sustainable systems on earth, but it was not the work of some outside artificial body or grand institutional design, but a system that started extremely small and has only ever grown from the energy - created by the process of photosynthesis - which is surplus to the requirements of the plant's survival. The rainforests **"obtain a yield"** and reinvests some of it to create sustainable growth

There is a word of caution here, however. This principle does not mean that money should be the prime motivator for all community efforts. Firstly, we've talked about other surpluses that can be used to grow other than money. Secondly, we've discussed how everything should always have at least two other functions beyond generating money. But, given the power of money, we should warn against distorting community efforts in pursuit of it. If you need a rule of thumb, money should only ever be a happy side effect, not the prime motivator. If in your mind an element of a design is not a success if no money is generated, then it probably highlights an area where you may have created liabilities and fragilities.

4. Catch and Store Energy

In Permaculture, this principle means to catch & store energy from the sun, wind, rain, as well as more abstract energy embodied in animals and humans. In community building, this has a number of meanings.

Firstly, it forces us to take an "asset-based" view of our community. It means we have to look for the gifts, skills and energy that exist within our own community, and which flow through it (for example, seasonal workers, students or tourists). In order to capture, store or utilise the benefits of energy flows, we must first see that there are benefits. This principle causes us to creatively work with nature, rather than against it.

Secondly, the directive to catch and store energy in community terms causes us to think about how we use that energy. If your area sees university students come & go throughout the year, you might see them as a problem to your community garden, because they aren't there all year round to take on responsibilities. However, if you understand this as a flow of energy, you can ensure that you don't extend beyond the capacity of the "troughs" but creatively use the "peaks" to your advantage. For example, you could plan bigger changes to coincide with the student year, perhaps investments that enable you to reduce your workload in the "troughs". In this way, you "store" the energy provided by this flow for the rest of the year.

Lastly, it brings us to the topic of funding. Funding does indeed represent energy that is flowing through communities, in the same way that the sun shines on our gardens. This directive <u>does</u> say that we should take advantage of external energy when it's available.

I have been critical of funding so far, for good reason. In Chapters 5 & 6, we looked at this more from the perspective of the "helper" who wanted to help by giving funding or external resources. Here, however, we are looking at the problem more from the perspective of whether citizens should ever take advantage of funding when it's available. The answer is yes, but with caution.

We should understand that funding is an energy flow - like seasonal rains and day & night - not a constant. Just like when we thought about flows of students as energy, funding should not be used for routine, day-to-day expenses, and it should be used with extreme caution to expand. Funding can be used, however, to cover extra, one-off, optional expenses and to invest in making the routine workings more efficient.

For example, a community garden could use funding in a number of ways, some conducive to sustainability, some not. For example:

- If the garden has grown (too fast, too large) to a point that in order to keep up with routine work, someone might need to be employed. But if the garden doesn't create the yield (money) for itself, it could use this funding (though by following these principles we can avoid being put in this situation in the first place). But the effect of using funding to employ someone (a routine, day-to-day expense) means that the garden becomes reliant on an uninterrupted flow of funding, which is going to create fragility and unsustainability.

- If the garden decides to use the funds to take on a new site, perhaps using it to pay the upfront costs of setting up the site, then it runs the risk of growing too fast, creating liabilities (i.e. requirements for future money & energy) that it cannot sustain, and collapsing either partially or totally. Despite the unsustainability this creates, this is primarily what I've seen funding used for. In the interests of sustainability - and ultimately, the community - I suggest avoiding using funding for these categories of expense.

- However, funding can be used sustainably too. It could pay for a consultant to look at the site and make suggestions, perhaps about efficiency. It could pay for *extra* manure or mulch that could add nutrients to the soil. It could pay for a one-off advertising campaign for extra volunteers. Or even better, perhaps it could pay for a huge party!

A good rule of thumb is that funding should be used for nice-to-haves, not need-to-haves.

When funding (or any intermittent, external flow of energy) is used for nice-to-haves and not need-to-haves - which should be "funded" from within (see "obtain a yield") - you can be more selective about the funding you receive, because you're not reliant on it. As we've discussed elsewhere, funding should be used to support you & your neighbours in doing what you want, not dictate your priorities. It should not turn your bumping space into a fixing space. It should not have targets for you to meet, especially if those targets require large & fast changes. It also should not require a disproportionate amount of energy to measure and write reports. And, just like building a system to rely on a perpetual summer or for a constant amount of rain, it is creating a huge liability to design a system to be reliant on a constant flow of external funding.

In this way, you can creatively and positively use the funding energy that exists around you in a way that benefits you without creating dependence on it.

5. Use & Value Renewable Resources

Building on this, we can get a little bit deeper than a simple dichotomy of "nice-to-haves" and "need-to-haves" and look at how we should prioritise how we spend resources in general.

Permaculture, in an ecological sense, deals with how we should "spend" our surplus energy in great nuance. In the Permaculture Designers Manual, Mollinson identifies 5 different grades of resources:

1. Those which increase by modest use
2. Those unaffected by use
3. Those which disappear or degrade if not used
4. Those reduced by use
5. Those which pollute or destroy other resources

His directive is that we should prioritise using resources in that order, and avoid Grade 5 altogether. Economics also identifies these categories but splits them in a less nuanced way - as "assets" (1-2) and "liabilities" (3-5). In a financial sense, assets are things that make money or retain value. In other words, an equal amount or more energy/money is derived from it than is spent in its purchase, creation or use. On the other hand, liabilities are things in which a lot of money and/or energy is lost in its use or lack of use without adequate return.

This analysis of different types of resources can also inform how we use resources in our community designs.

For example, we should prioritise resources that will only improve with time & use, such as creating a space where people can give their gifts (which will flourish with use), more skills & knowledge (which can be shared & strengthened in use) and connections (each connection begets further connections). When we create bumping spaces, it creates a snowball of energy that will only increase with use.

In contrast, external, institutional resources can be understood as Grade 4 at best - reduced by use - or Grade 5 - damaging to other resources (e.g. community connections & gifts of citizens).

6. Produce no waste

In permaculture, "work" (by a human) is needed because a need of an ecosystem is not met from within the system, while "waste" is an output of that ecosystem that is not being used productively by another element. Therefore, waste is seen as an opportunity to eliminate work (and financial expense, which is crystallised work). It is ensuring that there is a minimal need for external energy and a minimal loss of energy from the system.

In community terms, there is often a huge amount of waste from a community, which can take many forms.

Let's take money first. The problem of money leaving communities through its spending in chain shops has already been identified in many circles, and has led to the creation of some local currencies and an encouragement to "shop local". This spending can be viewed as "waste" in such a way as it is a missed opportunity to use that money within the system.

However, money can be wasted in other ways - alongside other things. Say your project needs some benches. However, instead of looking for unwanted benches in your community (using other people's waste), or the unwanted raw materials that could be upcycled by someone who has a gift for woodwork (a waste of someone's gifts, the raw materials and the opportunity for building knowledge, skills and connections in the process), you spend your limited money on it instead - wasting the money that should be saved for when there is no alternative.

This highlights some of the other ways we can create "waste", actively or passively (i.e. by ignoring), in our communities. When people's gifts go unused, that is waste. When opportunities for building connections are missed, that is waste. As well as the energy required to take physical waste away from a community when it could be used within that community.

Whenever we decide to create a change, we should always look for the resources in our community first, for many reasons, but if for no other reason than to reduce waste. Those resources could be an item (bench), raw materials (wood) or gifts & skills.

Furthermore, we waste energy by what I call "not completing the circle of giving & receiving".

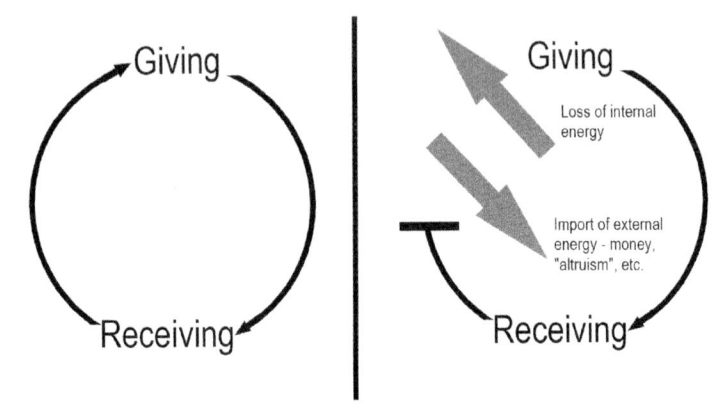

(Fig 4.) - Left: The cycle of giving & receiving is complete. Right: The cycle of giving & receiving is incomplete. Energy that could be recycled escapes the system, necessitating the system to be propped up by external energy.

When the circle is completed, there is no giving without also receiving, and no receiving without also giving. While also naturally flattening the hierarchy that we see in many charities where there are "givers" (volunteers & professionals) and "receivers" (clients, service users, etc.), I have also found it key for sustainability.

In many charity models, those who are receiving are prevented from giving, from contributing to their own solutions. The energy of the receivers is then wasted, while also creating an "energy gap" that must be filled by external energy, which is ultimately unsustainable and will eventually run out. The most common short-term stopgaps that are used is a sense of altruism or some sort of morality that compels people to give, as well as money and funding, which is either used to pay someone to fill the gap full-time or to import external energy in another way.

However, when the circle is completed, there is a natural sustainability. If you consider many non-traditional helping domains, for example, the family unit or the friendship group, through the framework of the circle of giving and receiving, you'll see that it naturally does this.

By allowing people to contribute to their own solutions in whatever way aligns with their gifts, the energy that is gained by receiving is "recycled" back into the system as giving. Those that give away their energy also have it replenished by receiving.

Consider an example of a food bank versus a community-led food project. A food bank has a sharp dichotomy of givers and receivers. There are those that work in the warehouse and/or deliver food (in some schemes, especially during COVID) who are "giving" their energy away for moral or altruistic reasons (or perhaps for more personal reasons, as considered in the chapter on the "Through" road) but are not using food bank food to feed themselves, and so they are in some sort of energy deficit. Meanwhile, there are those that receive the food who are considered by the food bank to have nothing to give, to have no useful gifts. They are often prevented from giving their energy and gifts to the food bank and society. The rigid, bureaucratic nature of many food banks can't make use of the talented chef, the gifted poet, the green-fingered gardener or the avid cyclist. They don't use the surplus energy from the system to create food sovereignty and reinvest energy back into the system. Many food banks, therefore, run on a perpetual energy gap, with the gap being made up by altruistic shoppers, donators, volunteers and funding. However, the moment their source of external energy fails, the food bank will collapse.

In contrast, in a community-led food project, there is no difference between giver and receiver. Those that pick up the food from the supermarket also feed themselves using that food. Receivers contribute their gifts - the chef cooks up the surplus food once a month, where the poet performs while everyone is eating. The artist makes beautiful signs for the event. The community made a bike trailer for the avid cyclist to pick up food from a farm shop out of town. They started small and only grew as surplus energy became available, feeding more and more people, but those extra people didn't require more external energy to be imported <u>because they bring their own energy with them.</u> Beyond just balancing giving and receiving, my experience is that completing the circle of giving and receiving creates

<u>surplus</u> energy which can be reinvested in the system for growth.

The principle underlying this is that each person will, for the most part, give and receive in equal amounts, in their own way that aligns with their gifts. A project only requires external energy - funding and altruism - when they close off part of that cycle with misplaced ideas about paternalism and mistrust.

7. Use & Value Diversity

This is an important directive in so many respects because it actually goes completely against the current paradigm, which says that there is only ever one "right way", one "standard", one "truth". It says that there is one state of health, one "healthy" body type, one standard of behaviour etc. Some extremists even go so far as to say that there is only one correct skin colour. We can see this everywhere that people apply their own standards & values to other people, thinking that the world would be right if everyone did something or other. In our current age, this paradigm is undergoing modification to include greater "tolerance" of difference, but it is <u>only a modification</u>.

This principle is entirely different and is crucially important for sustainable community building. It says that we should <u>use & value</u> diversity. This goes beyond simply *accepting* diversity, but embracing it and using it positively.

The most sustainable projects will use & value the diversity in their communities, beyond the normal tokenistic concepts like "difference of opinion". For example, they will understand the value of different approaches to work - those that like to work and not talk, and those that like to mainly talk while working, and those that only want to talk and not "work". It is beyond toleration of difference, it is using it positively and embracing it.

It also helps us reduce conflict in our communities. We often think there's one way to achieve something, and we get annoyed when people don't believe us, join us, or actively do the opposite. But when we realise that the truth is usually somewhere in the middle and that natural selection will choose between one and another for us, then we can see the value of a diversity of approaches, as it gives the best chance of a good approach being the one that survives, rather than the lesser evil of two or none at all.

Truth is found in diversity. It's probable that I will be proved wrong in at least some things that I've written in this book, probably all of it, especially with the passage of time. Even if writing this isn't valuable to the search for truth because what I say is right, it is valuable because it contributes to diversity. It helps us find the truth, even if I'm totally wrong. I'm also not trying to convince anybody. Because of diversity, some will resonate with this, some will not. That's fine, I'm only out to give energy to those who resonate with this.

This is important to community building because it allows us to seek out, use and benefit from diversity in our communities and helps us peacefully co-exist with or even complement & help other approaches.

A further extension of this principle of seeing the value in diversity **is that all critical functions should be supported in a diversity of ways (in the Permaculture world, at least 3).**

This means that when someone is employed by a project - the provision of a wage becoming a critical function - then funding should at least only be only one way that we support that wage. With three ways to support each critical function, we cannot help but design in sustainability. This counters the traditional path that reduces the support of a critical function to a minimum in the name of "efficiency".

8. Integrate, don't segregate

Linked to using & valuing diversity is the principle to "integrate, not segregate". This is again the opposite of the traditional way of doing things, where we segregate people by their problems into services. In ABCD, we integrate diversity instead, by linking people who share passions or gifts but are geographically diverse, or are geographically in the same place but have diverse gifts.

When planning your community design, there is strength & resilience in integrating functions over segregating them. Let's just look at the GP surgery, which is currently segregated to fulfil one function - a place for people to go and seek advice from a health care professional, while other functions reside elsewhere. But why does the GP surgery just have to be for in-hours medicine? Could it also provide a bumping space for neighbours or host other activities? Could the waiting room be a connection space/café as well as a waiting room? Could a café fund the initiatives that come out of the neighbours meeting in the waiting room? "Social Prescribers" and "Link Workers" are hidden in an office, doling out appointments and advice when real "community animators" are in the waiting room connecting neighbours. Could the rooms be used for something else in the evenings? Could the GP surgery be incorporated into other structures that the neighbours already use? The possibilities are endless.

This again reminds us that **every element in a design should have at least three functions**, if not more.

9. Use Edges & Value the Marginal

An "Edge" in Permaculture is the boundary between two mediums - for example, the boundary between the soil and the air, or the sea and the land. It is well recognised that the edge is a zone of high energy transfer between the two mediums, such that scientific samples intentionally avoid the edge because they are atypical. In Permaculture, rather than seeing the edge as atypical & problematic, we take advantage of its high energy flow. For example, permaculturists will design vegetable beds with lots of zigs & zags rather than straight lines to maximise the length of the edge and take advantage of that energy transfer.

We see the value of the edge in the human sphere too. Social edge is created any time two people meet - and the more diverse the two people are, the more powerful is the edge (reminding us of using & valuing diversity).

It is well recognised by historians of the Industrial Revolution that inventions & progress occurred most not where people were best educated or even where the necessity was greatest, but where the greatest number of diverse industries were co-located. Through the mixing of these different industries (over a beer in the pub perhaps), a solution that had long been applied in one industry was tweaked to solve a problem in a different industry, and so on.

In our community designs, we should always seek to maximise social edge, building on using & valuing diversity and integration. When we bring together (integrate) a workshop project and a garden project, or we introduce two neighbours, we increase the edge in our community and beautiful things grow out of this energetic edge.

"The Marginal" is what exists at the edge of our community. This returns to ideas of using & valuing diversity - we often assume that the only things that have value are what is at the centre of our community. However, this principle directs us to value what is at the edge. People are marginalised and pushed out to the edges of community, but that doesn't mean they don't have value. It is true that communities should be able to welcome these marginalised people back into the centre of the community if those people want ("Welcoming the Stranger" in ABCD-talk), but this should also not be a precondition of value or a moral imperative. Some people may choose to be at the edge of community - travellers & nomads for example - or even at the edge of organisations, and they should be valued as masters of Edge. In a community sense, I often refer to these people - myself included - as "pollinators", never being at the centre of a community or organisation, but moving between communities and organisations, bringing with them the pollen, manipulating edge. In ages past, these pollinators were travelling storytellers, and in our modern mobile age, we should not lament that there are not more people at the heart of community, but celebrate the increased cross-pollination of travellers and increased edge.

People who have been labelled out of communities also have value. They have lived experience of working with institutions and with other people who have been labelled out of community. If they want to be, they would be masters at walking along the edges of community and weaving connections from the centre to the edge, and across boundaries.

While there should always be a place in the heart of community for those that want it and for those pollinators who decide to "settle down", those at the edges of community shouldn't be assumed valueless if they don't come into the centre. We should use edge & value the marginal.

10. Accept feedback & apply self-regulation

In nature, plants have no huge brains like humans, but the ecosystems made up of those plants have an emergent property of self-regulation, almost as if the system itself had intelligent thought. Self-regulation is an emergent property. Nature will use pioneer species - what we call "weeds" - which are well adapted to extreme conditions to repair damaged soil. When we "weed", we should understand we are interfering with nature's healing process (There is an analogy here to communities). Even in healthy systems, like the rainforest, there is a continual loop of feedback and adaptation from all sources. If something is out of balance, then other things will adapt. Populations of prey and predator will fluctuate, but will generally stay in balance over the long term.

In community systems, however, we often find that, despite our obsession with measuring certain outcomes, we actually ignore most feedback and interfere with the community's attempt at self-regulation.

What is the likely response of a project with falling volunteer numbers? It is likely to spend a disproportionate amount of the community's resources on "advertising" to try to reverse that trend. However, if we accept it as feedback and self-regulation, we can see that this is the community voting with its feet and natural selection at work. Perhaps the organisation has become too "fix-y", artificial and rigid thanks to external influence, and the time has come to allow it to pass so that it creates a niche of time & space in which a better community solution can grow. Perhaps the function that it served is no longer relevant. We should work with nature, not against it. In Part 1, we also looked at an example of how this principle worked with institutions trying to "manage" demand rather than accepting feedback. Accept feedback & apply self-regulation.

However, humans have an ability that goes beyond the meta-brain of communities, in that we can make conscious decisions. Much of the work in community associations is about decision making, and this principle helps us understand how this should be made. Every citizen in a community, every member of an association, is the most sensitive feedback component in any system. This is the opposite of traditional approaches, where citizens or members are assumed to be the least knowledgeable about the state of the system, which then leads to taking the "Through" road ("we know best if only they'd just do what we say!). When we see that citizens are the closest to the system and are therefore the most intuitively knowledgeable about the state of the system (they might not know numbers, but they sure as hell still know what their community wants), it inevitably leads to citizen-led approaches like ABCD.

This principle directs us to use this to our advantage. Decision making should be decentralised as much as possible and should always be democratic. Participatory decision making is preferred over representative decision making. And when citizens tell you something - verbally or with their feet - then they know what they're doing. They are the instruments of a community's self-regulation.

It also means that we should look for validation from within our communities, rather than from outside bodies or measurements against external standards.

11. Creatively use & respond to change

Building on the above principle, when change happens, we should respond creatively and use it to its advantage, rather than attempting to fight change. One of the favourite phrases of permaculturists is that **"the problem is the solution"**. When nature attempts to heal itself, it will use a succession of solutions - beginning with pioneer species ("weeds") which then create the conditions for other species, which then create the conditions for other species, until returning to "balance". In this way, nature is homeostatic (balance-seeking), just like the body, although over such a long time frame that it is difficult for humans to observe. By fighting these changes, we can be interfering with the natural healing process of nature.

Change always happens in communities too, and usually for good reason. Perhaps the priority of the community right now is localising food production to meet food needs, but perhaps when that has been achieved, the priority is felt to be supporting children to play. Perhaps this will lead to the shrinking of associations dedicated to the growth of food production. The traditional paradigm will cause us to lament the loss of these associations, and even label those nominally in charge of having done a bad job. However, we should celebrate and use change positively and creatively.

12. Create bumping spaces

This one is not based on a permaculture principle, but I think that this is the most important principle of community building and deserves to be the one on which we finish.

Positive change happens in communities through connection, and the prime directive when intervening in community space should not be to try to solve the problem directly but by creating the conditions in which your community can solve it. Bumping spaces can take all different forms, and is anywhere that edge is created. We should focus not on forcing our neighbours to care about X issue, get funding for Y or create Z, but connect our neighbours so that they can do it themselves.

In the same way that we cannot doing the physical growing of plants, instead we create a space with the conditions in which plants grow naturally, so too can we not do the physical growing of communities, but we can create the spaces in which connections happen and community grows spontaneously. Bumping spaces can take many forms, but the best bumping spaces have no agenda, no fixing and are fully accessible. I feel my next major piece of writing will focus on bumping spaces.

Chapter 10:
What do communities create?

So far, we've referred to communities as complex adaptive systems. There is no set definition of a CAS, but key characteristics are:

- A network of relationships between components
- Individual components that adapt & learn
- The network works together for a purpose e.g. to create something or to serve a function
- The function or product isn't necessarily obvious from the behaviour of the individual components

So some examples of natural CASs are neurons of the brain which create consciousness or an ant colony that works together to ensure mutual survival. Without these "products" or functions, they are simply networks, not systems. So what is the "product" or "function" of community? Well, humans suck at surviving on their own. The product of community, in its most abstract form, is simply to better ensure the survival of its members (specifically, the progeny of its members). Human beings, having always existed in tribes, have clearly evolved complex mechanisms over the years, and those with the best mechanisms have been selected for and have taken over the globe to the extent we see today.

Short of this most abstract form - raw survival - there are several "subgoals" that are more familiar to us because we discuss these subgoals all the time. Without serving these functions, the human community could not survive very long. The list may well be endless and can certainly be debated, however, Cormac Russell in "Rekindling Democracy" and John McKnight in "The Abundant Community" highlight seven functions of community they have observed:

- They keep us healthy (see later chapter on health)
- They support a local formal (i.e. financial) economy, creating jobs, trade etc.
- They help raise children
- They feed people (i.e. local food production)
- They care when it's needed (e.g. in old age)
- They keep us safe
- They ensure ecological sustainability

They observe that these are functions that well-connected communities spontaneously fulfil, and better than an institution could possibly achieve. The better connected, the better the community fulfils the function. To a large extent, however, seeing these as functions that communities fulfil is only one way of looking at it. The upside is that it's easy to understand, and that's really important. The downside is that it doesn't necessarily explain the relationship to connection and why these functions couldn't necessarily be carried out mechanically by institutions or by individuals.

Another way of viewing this is through the lens of emergence. Though more difficult to understand, it explains some of these questions that appear when we dig.

When looking at a group of things, their "properties" can be split into either collective properties or emergent properties. Collective properties are the aggregation of individual properties - for example, the average age of the group, or the percentage of males or females. Emergent properties are properties that arise only at the level of the group. For example, a collective property of the brain might be the percentage of neurons firing at any one time, but an emergent property might be consciousness - a property that can't be said to exist for neurons. A collective property of lots of brains might be average IQ, but an emergent property is the progression of human knowledge.

Change at the level of the community

In the same way, the aforementioned seven functions are properties that can only be created by communities, not by individual humans - or at least, the way it exists for an individual person is qualitatively different. Despite this, these properties are actually most often viewed as *collective,* for example*:*

- Average life expectancy or prevalence of disease
- Incidence of crime
- Number of single-parent families
- Percentage unemployment
- Biodiversity measurements

Thus, the problem and the solution is reduced to the level of the person, often in a deficit focused way:

- A person who needs to make better lifestyle choices
- A person in need of rehabilitation from a criminal mindset
- A person who needs to make better environmental choices

But if we see the issues we often care about - safety, environmental sustainability, raising children - as being *emergent* properties then we see that the problem and solution are actually to be found at the level of the community, not the level of individuals.

This has already been said in multiple ways by astute observers throughout the ages: it takes a village to raise a child; we don't have a health problem, we have a village one (Cormac Russell); change best happens at the scale of the neighbourhood. Through emergent properties, we can find a scientific understanding for these empirical observations.

Understood as emergent properties, we also understand two more critical characteristics. They are created unconsciously by the "components of the system" (i.e. citizens in a community) and the degree of connection between components is important to the relative strength of the emergent property.

Unconscious actions

This theme that has emerged throughout the book is that actually the vast majority of the work that creates wellbeing, happiness, safety, security & sustainability is done entirely unconsciously by actors who have almost no intention to or knowledge that they are creating those properties.

As mentioned in the section on the "unconscious citizen", when we give someone a lift, we're not necessarily considering sustainability. When we let someone know about a job vacancy you heard about or when we lend someone a tool, you're not considering creating security (of access to resources) in the community.

This is completely opposite to the conventional view of the way these properties are created e.g. health is created by health care professionals and people choosing to live a healthy lifestyle. Meanwhile, going to a pub with a friend is not considered to be "health creation" and we don't see public health programs to enable people to go to the pub & socialise, even though the effect of social connections or loneliness on health is well documented. Apparently, sustainability is created by people making good moral choices to recycle or take public transport, but not by people who give their neighbours a surplus courgette or replacing their driveway with a lawn. They say safety is created by police officers and the justice system but not by neighbours who know each other's names or house-sit for eachother.

I hope by now the point is self-evident. We only need to look into our lives for all the countless, unconscious ways normal, uncredentialed people have made us safer, healthier or happier. That's not to deny the role of professionals and institutions, but that at the very least a significant role is played by unconscious actors changes the overall practical understanding of how these functions are filled.

Assuming that health, security, care and sustainability are created consciously leads to the idea that safety is created by "safety specialists" as predictably as cars are made by car specialists and watches by watch specialists. It puts professionals & institutions in the lead. It puts the "For" and "Through" roads at the fore, as well as the idea that citizens should defer to expert judgement and do what they're told when in contact with professionals, and live their lives in a conscientious, disciplined fashion when not.

However, even if we just admit a significant role for unconscious actors, let alone if we take it to be the vast majority, this changes things. If these properties are created unconsciously, they are emergent properties as a result of self-organising citizens.

Connection

If these properties are the result of self-organising systems, then connection is a key factor, and I think, at least currently, the primary limiting factor to communities being able to create security, health, safety and more.

It would almost be impossible to measure, but I would hypothesise that if you could quantify connection in community, you would find a correlation with all these properties. The closest we have are studies into loneliness and its effect on health, the effect of associational life on health and the effect of knowing your neighbours' name on safety.

Linked to this is a further property of communities as a complex adaptive system, which is that they self-heal. Community connections have been damaged by capitalism & by institutions, however, unconscious community connectors are the community's own self-healing mechanisms, repairing these connections and reweaving. Community Animators can further catalyse this process. By recognising that communities know how to self-heal, it directs us to not interfere with that process from outside.

Chapter 11:
Health & Healthism

There are two reasons why I'm going to single out health to discuss. Before that, though, I want to highlight that this discussion around health is not about the healthcare system or the process of reversing or alleviating disease - this is a book in itself. This analysis will focus on health and how it is created in the community, and is a critique of health care in so far as they reach into this space. This isn't about critiquing or attempting to reform the healthcare system, but the whole discourse around health, which has more application to the way in which health promotion or public health is carried out.

The first reason is that because I have a background and special interest in health. As a result of this, I haven't spent the time & energy on other subjects that would justify me writing a chapter on it. I leave the space free and look forward to others with a special interest in safety & crime, economics, education and others going in-depth in those subject areas.

The second is that rhetoric about health is all-pervasive. Almost everyone & everything claims to promote health, yet it is a vague concept that lacks definition. However, while we all pretend that pursuing health is the noblest of causes and free of criticism, those standards of health are actually used to beat down & oppress certain groups of people - for example, fatphobia & healthism.

I hope one day to expand this chapter into a book of its own, it certainly deserves it. Here, I just hope this chapter enables those of us who subscribe to the values espoused in this book to apply them to the realm of health and pivot away from healthism and towards empowerment. I hope it also provides concepts, language & tools to those who are forced to fight for their right to eschew institutional labels of health and individually define what health means to them. I stand beside you.

Who gets to define what health is?

Health is a slippery concept, and most would agree that there is no one definition that people agree with. Is it just the absence of disease, or is it something more than that? Rather than write a treatise offering my feeble attempt to define health, we can look one order higher and ask what I think is the most important question: who has the power to define "health".

In our current society, those who predominantly get to define health are professionals and those working in institutions - doctors, academics, politicians - or really anyone except the individual that the health definition affects. What this definition is actually composed of changes over time, but it is always an <u>institutional definition of health</u>. Whatever the result of their inquiries, all institutional definitions of health share common characteristics. Firstly, as mentioned, they derive from outside the individual person. Secondly, they attempt to define health objectively, meaning that one standard of health is true for all humans.

Despite all the rhetoric around "personalisation", "what is important for the individual" and "empowerment", rarely or never do individuals get to actually define what health actually is for themselves. They might be given the freedom to pick & choose which bits of the institutional health definition is most important to them at the time, but never do they actually get to redefine the measures of health dictated by professionals. That power is reserved by the elite to administer "benevolently" onto the masses. An individual's definition of health is necessarily subjective, not objective. No two people's definition of what health is for them can be the same.

So who is right? I believe all the same arguments as I set out about who knows what their system needs best still apply - the one closest to the feedback, the person educated by experience in the particular, the person themself vs. or the one educated by books in the general. We are all complex beings with highly sophisticated mechanisms of homeostasis, and to believe that an outsider can accurately direct that homeostasis better than the person themself is self-evidently laughable.

The purpose of this chapter, however, is not to convince those who believe in the institutional definition of health, or that the most educated know best while ordinary people don't know what's good for them, to start thinking that the individual, subjective definition of health is more correct. The purpose is to help people who already believe in the values set out here, in ABCD, in citizen-led change, to apply those values to the field of health, and in so doing, become allies to those who are fighting for their right to define what health means for them, and to live a life without judgement. Institutional definitions of health are so omnipresent and subtle, that many who are the world's best advocates for individuals defining their own good life swallow & promote wholesale the institutional health narrative.

Institutional Definitions of Health

Institutions & professionals attempt to create objective criteria by which "health" can be assessed. This objective definition is also an exclusive one, dividing bodies, minds, people, food, behaviours and bodily sensations into two categories: "healthy" and "unhealthy". The current trend for what institutions define as health is:

- Absence of disease
- We should eat "healthy" foods and avoid "unhealthy" ones - though this definition changes frequently. Where once this was about "dieting", it has now morphed into "lifestyle changes".
- We should eat according to certain rules - when, where, how much, at what frequency, what quality etc. - as prescribed by those who know best (though again, these change frequently).
- We should move our bodies in certain ways called "exercise" (other sorts of movement don't qualify) at intensities & frequencies prescribed by those who know best (this also changes frequently)
- We should use both the above in an attempt to manipulate the size of our bodies (the desirable size being subject to much change throughout history)
- We should avoid "unhealthy" substances like alcohol, tobacco & certain illegal drugs
- We should engage in certain activities that promote "mental health" and "resilience" like mindfulness, green activities and resilience workshops.
- We should always consult professionals about our problems

- We should follow the advice of professionals in these consultations to the letter
- We should worry about being physiologically out of "limits" and do everything we can to fit within them

The implication in all of these things is that there is a healthy way to choose to live, and an unhealthy one (not doing the above or, god forbid, doing the opposite), and that by living a "healthy" lifestyle, you <u>will</u> have a better life. It is blasphemy to suppose that doing what the institution defines as "unhealthy" could actually be in someone's best interests. Certainly, those of us who dare to question institutional health mandates are treated as heretics.

<u>Mapping onto the Helper's Crossroads</u>

Any time someone's health, good life or route to homeostasis is defined by an external body or professional (Illich called this "heteronomous direction of homeostasis"), it falls into the top row of our crossroads: the "To", "For" and "Through" road. Much of medicine - both curative & preventative - appears to sit in the realm of "For". This can be cast into doubt, however, when we look at historical definitions of health (e.g. to be a heterosexual or a passive woman) and how definitions of health have been used to further the priorities of those doing the defining throughout history ("To"). When we look back at today's definition of health from the future, particularly the modern obsession with weight &

body size, will we still see our current picture of health as being beneficent ("For") or will we with the benefit of hindsight & progress, see the way this definition was used to further other ends ("To")?

Medicine has long recognised, though, that it has only a limited ability on the "For" road to influence those factors that it defines as health. This found renewed strength in the recent popularity of the concept of "Social Determinants of (Institutional) Health". The Social Determinants of Institutional Health basically detail a variety of factors outside of healthcare systems that determine around 80% of our health. But rather than recognising that these social determinants represent the huge diversity of approaches that individual people use to create health for themselves, they have mistakenly seen it as just further modifiable components that both institutions and communities can use to better promote institutional priorities. Rather than understanding that this undermined their model, they expanded it to tolerate it.

This has led in recent times to a significant push to relocate functions that have been in the institutional realm into the community sphere. This has been assumed to be universally a good thing, and indeed, there are benefits to doing so, but what has been missing from the analysis so far is how the power to define what a good, healthy life looks like has been retained by the institution.

Predominantly until now, institutions have done nothing more than outsource their work to volunteer community groups, while continuing to try to manipulate the community to meet the institution's priorities - the "Through" road. This is not about empowering or building community. In fact, it could even be viewed as exploiting community labour to achieve your objectives. This is very different from the "With" and "By" road, which would involve decentralising the power to communities and individuals to define what needs to happen for them to be healthy, or indeed, the choice not to pursue health at all.

Healthism

The "Through" road can be a particularly dangerous road to walk, and nowhere is this currently more obvious than in health. Anytime we talk about community engagement, promotion, or ask questions like "why don't they care?" or "if only more people could be bothered to do X", this is a red flag that we're taking the "Through" road. The answer to these questions is "*because* you're on the "Through" road". They are red flags that we are forcing our priorities or values onto another person and getting annoyed or confused that they don't care about our values as much as we do. When we allow people to act on their own priorities and values, to define the problem, there is never a need for questions like this.

Due to the overwhelming power of health institutions and narratives, it has created "Healthism" to recruit citizens & communities to its cause. Healthism is an "ism" in both senses of the word. In the -ism sense like "Utilitarianism" or "Fascism", it is a philosophy that preaches that the only way to a good life is to relentlessly pursue a handful of narrow criteria as defined by professionals & specialists. It is exclusive when it says that people who have a larger or different body, who have a long term condition or a mental health problem cannot live a good life until they first solve those problems. Within this all-pervasive paradigm, these people are not allowed to be healthy or happy. We can begin to get an idea of who these standards benefit when we consider that the resources necessary to achieve this "good life" are accessible to only a small portion of society (and that's before we consider genetic diversity) and that the path to a good life ensures the continued need for institutions and professionals.

When we start to see this as a specific model, rather than the universally accepted truth that it feels like when growing up in Western society, we see the philosophy of "healthism" everywhere, particularly in advertising and in the helping spaces. We turn up at the Helper's Crossroads, wondering how we might help, and the easy answer is to assume for others that their best life is to be found in the pursuit of the institutional, healthist definition of health, without giving them space to define what a good life means to them. It's important to note here that what I'm saying is not that we should accept that some people don't want to be healthy or choose to have some unhealthy characteristics - this is covered by traditional "autonomy" in medical ethics - but that people can be healthy regardless of how well they fit the institutional model of health, and can become healthy (in the true, holistic sense) by doing things the institutional model of health considers unhealthy.

The other really dangerous aspect of healthism is the second sense of 'ism' - as in "racism" or "sexism". Healthism not only recruits us to spend our own lives in pursuit of its goals rather than our own, but also to police our neighbours' health. The Biocitizenship Paradigm is well established in Western society and causes us to use institutional definitions of health and "burden" on nationalised services as barometers by which to measure the "goodness" or "badness" of our neighbours. Fat people are particularly targeted with fatphobia and healthism and are excluded socially in many ways for being born in a bigger body.

And what we do to each other, we also do to ourselves. So much of our emotional energy & time is spent distancing ourselves from our own internal homeostatic cues (our thoughts & feelings) and instead trying to "discipline" ourselves to live, eat, exercise, rest and sleep according to external rules set by professionals who profess to know better than your body what your body needs. Then, when our body's needs cannot stand being ignored anymore, we call it "falling off the wagon" and punish ourselves. We spend our entire lives yo-yoing between restriction and binge (to balance extreme restriction, we need an extreme binge, and we don't allow ourselves to restore to a more natural balance). Our self-image, too, becomes tied to how well we fulfil these external rules rather than how well we listen to our own needs.

This is only a small introduction to healthism, and is intended to show how healthism is incorporated into the Helper's Crossroads model, and to introduce community folk to the concept. If you intend to work in health, I strongly recommend the scholarship of many fat activists and healthism thinkers whose analysis and lived experience of healthism far outstrip mine. To not understand healthism is to do tremendous harm to society.

So what's the alternative to healthism?

If we truly want to help improve someone's health, we have to remove all notions of what we think "health" means, and allow the person to define what it means for them. In this way, the word "health" or "healthy" can actually be unhelpful because of the way that deep-seated beliefs about health obscure things not traditionally considered health creating.

If we truly want to improve someone's health, we have to respect what their homeostatic impulses are telling them. Ivan Illich suggested that "health levels can only decline when survival comes to depend beyond a certain point on heteronomous (other-directed) regulation of the organism's homeostasis".

This includes where they might have what are usually termed "unhealthy coping mechanisms". If we use the "Social Determinants of Health" in an inclusive way, as the "Social Determinants of Subjective Health", we can see that almost anything that someone pursues because they feel it matters is health-promoting. There are not just "Five Ways to Well-Being". There are infinite.

Community-created health

When we remove our institutional spectacles and stop limiting what we consider healthy according to narrow, pre-defined criteria, then we can see the vast amounts that communities actually contribute to the creation of health. If our internal SatNav is always pointing us towards health, homeostasis or resilience to external causes of unbalance, then our health is only limited by our capacity to act on those internal directions: the "General Resistance Resources" of Antonovsky's "Salutogenesis". Much of the "resources" or "assets" that determine the capacity to meet our needs do not lie within the individual, but within the community. Therefore it's impossible to think of the health of a person in isolation from their community.

People who live in "friendly", well-connected communities will find it easier to meet their need for socialising than those who live isolated, in disconnected ones. People who live in a well-connected community with an active gift economy will find it easier to meet their need for a job, housing or food, especially in periods of scarcity that would be detrimental to health in disconnected communities.

The interface between the individual and the community "health" resources occurs via millions of small, unconscious, informal and uncontracted actions. It is having a cup of tea or going for a walk with a friend, it is the ability to find some people to have a kick about with, it is having a friend to text when you feel crap. It is hand-me-down clothes and toys from friends. It is your friends keeping their eye out for jobs. It is staying with a friend for a few nights between tenancies. As much as institutions might try to ape these interactions, they are not the same as being in a true community.

To improve health, what we really need to do is to respect a person's own definition of their health, and do everything we can to increase their capacity to do what they need to meet that need. This can include using institutional resources when invited, but far more powerful is through helping them to have plentiful links to the informal gift economy in their community that we all use to support our own health unconsciously.

Community-ism

There is a very real danger that faces ABCD, and that is community-ism. Like healthism, it is the moral obligation and the value judgments we enforce on our neighbours to pursue the same things that we believe are right and valuable. In this case, however, it is being a good neighbour, getting involved in neighbour events or going out and building community. This is community-ism, and comes with all the same harms that healthism does.

Some people might not find value in connecting with their neighbours at this point in time, and that's okay. Some people might have the desire but not have the mental, time or financial capacity to do so at this point, and that's okay. Some people might have had their fingers burned by so-called "community" in the past, and that's okay. And you & your neighbours might not yet be offering something interesting to that person yet, and that's okay. Use and value diversity.

True community building, "With" or "By" road change & connection cannot take place within community-ism. Community-ism is outsiders setting the agenda of neighbourliness. We must be extremely mindful when we discuss community that we do not set up moral standards by which we judge our neighbours, or to attempt to guilt, cajole or otherwise manipulate our neighbours into being "good community folk".

Chapter 12: Social Prescribing

"Social Prescribing" is one of the biggest shifts in the way the NHS works with communities in many decades, and as such is worthy of attention. This is especially the case when some of its more outspoken proponents claim that social prescribing is the pinnacle of community building, or even that, in its current form, it represents asset-based community development.

Despite obvious concerns with the name, Social Prescribing is an excellent institutional reform, and will help a great many people. It has many limitations, however. Using the Helper's Crossroads map, we can figure out these limitations.

The Story

As we've just discussed in the last chapter, plenty of healthcare professionals (and others) have long recognised the role that community plays in health - the "social determinants of health". Independently in a number of places, community connectors - people working on the "By" road - found partnerships with innovative local institutions (predominantly GP surgeries but also others) who saw the positive effect these community connectors were having in their community. In these partnerships, working on the "With" road now, community connectors became paid and institutions could help people they cared about, especially people whose predominant relationships were with the institution, to reconnect to their communities in a way that professionals couldn't.

This mix of community connectors & community animators, paid by institutions but working in the community, was, as far as I can tell, very successful, especially in taking the most institutionalised, excluded and labelled, those often at the most extreme end of economic oppression, and using a mixture of community & institutional assets to reweave their connection to the community, understanding that those that they are helping have gifts that are needed by their community. They also were able to prevent institutionalisation to some extent by providing a non-institutional "referral" option for solutions that would normally be dealt with by a "To/For" solution. In this organic form, I would accept that link workers were working in an ABCD-informed way.

Unfortunately, as often happens in this space, social prescribing became a victim of its own success, because it attracted the eyes of the NHS. It became incorporated in the NHS Long Term and was rolled out across the NHS system - social prescribing link workers for every Primary Care Network. It was scaled up.

The Shift from "With" to "Through"

Here, something almost imperceptible occurred about the 'feel' of social prescribing to "gappers" and community connector link workers alike. It took on an institutional vibe, became rigid and artificial. Using the Helper's Crossroads, we can now understand the transition that Social Prescribing underwent, and understand its effects.

We've already watched as community connectors - working on the "By" road - were identified by small institutions such as GP surgeries and were brought onto the "With" road, while continuing to create the conditions for "By". But perhaps what wasn't understood was *why* this was working. It seems that it was simply assumed that by just getting the community involved as a "referral pathway", health was created. But from the Helper's Crossroads, we can see that the real critical factor was that people were given the power to define health for themselves and were supported with both institutional resources ("With") and through connection to the community to increase their capacity for health ("By").

For example, when the issue wasn't really asthma, but damp in their house, the GP surgery was able to use its institutional resources to press the council to take action. While personally observing the team at Hope Citadel Healthcare, a defining time in my life, I watched as the GP surgery supported their community to define the issues and watched the GPs and "Focused Care Workers" bend over backwards to support them. It wasn't all perfect - there was still some institutional setting of health goals - but I watched as the mixed team of doctors, nurses, receptionists and others genuinely cared and believed in their patients' own health-defining capacity.

The rollout, however, involved the introduction of targets, measurements and, most importantly, institutional definitions of health (see the previous chapter for more on this). The whole point of social prescribing stopped being to reweave relationships in community (with any "health" benefit being a happy, but almost unintended, side-effect) and became directly about improving health.

The link worker in this model becomes another health professional, performing an assessment to seek out institutional "social diagnoses" such as loneliness, unemployment, mental health problems or other "social determinants of institutional health" and attempting to prescribe a solution - be that an institution such as a service ("To/For") or a community one such as an association ("Through"), and all the second-order effects we discussed in Part 1.

We cannot call this ABCD or even ABCD-informed. We certainly cannot call this community work to any extent. When organisations are seeking institutional goals such as "health", they are automatically in opposition to the community. This is not deinstitutionalisation and de-labelling, but institutionalisation and labelling, but with new labels. I cannot understate the harm to communities that the claim that Social Prescribing is about community has created. The loss of thousands of natural community connectors who have been recruited by institutions and oriented to recruit their neighbours to pursue the institution's goals over their own will cause irrevocable harm to communities trying to self-heal from the countless insults that they have already suffered.

There is a lot of discussion about whether "Social Prescribing" is an appropriate name. The argument is that it is medicalising and institutionalising community work. I don't agree, because as I've demonstrated here, the community element has all but been erased from Social Prescribing, leaving the name as a very appropriate name for how it actually functions now. The NHS has birthed a totally new professional field, one whose remit goes far further than medical fields, and in fact, according to "social determinant of institutional health" theory, has no outer boundary, and intending to further colonise community space to further the aims of the NHS, "health" being one amongst them.

Recently, the next logical conclusion of social prescribing has revealed itself, the "Health & Wellbeing Coach" under the slogan of personalised care. Job descriptions for this role are often exactly the same as that of a Social Prescribing Link Worker, the primary difference being the population focus. At the least, I think the name is more honest about the intentions of social prescribing. The Health & Wellbeing Coach is supposed to be about personalised care, but various adverts for it are explicitly about improving health, reducing pharmaceutical wastage, the burden on the NHS or other institutional goals. This is much more explicitly "Through" road help.

This ties in with the healthism discussed in the previous chapter. Of course, none of this is mal-intentioned, but institutions are very subtle in the ways that they recruit citizens to jump on board with their goals. The Social Prescribing Link Worker and the Health & Wellbeing Coach are new, subtle, friendly-faced ways to replace the older ways that have already been demolished by gappers, anti-fatphobia and healthism activists.

This chapter also demonstrates how subtle the lines that separates the roads can be. Simply by orienting the help and support provided towards meeting institutional goals, it completely changes the outcomes involved. Remember that the difference between "With" and

"Through" is almost nothing more than supporting someone even when you think they're wrong.

What is the future of Social Prescribing?

Is there a world in which the current social prescribing infrastructure can do good? Yes.

"With" road partnerships, supporting community animators in the medical space to reweave, deinstitutionalise and de-label is a good thing. With careful allocation of institutional resources and prudence to not overreach, community animators can act as a catalyst to the community self-healing process.

To achieve this, Social Prescribing needs to urgently reverse the professionalisation of community connectors, stop putting barriers in their way, and empower link workers to practice the art that they're already exceptional at, the reason they were recruited, the very thing that they wanted the job for in the first place: being in their communities helping, connecting & empowering. They need to be given power to help in counterintuitive (to the institution) ways, led by the person & community they're trying to help. Measuring performance by measures such as "reduced 999 calls", "reduced emergency admissions", "reduced GP appointments", "reduced pharmaceutical wastage" or others is distorting as all of those things might even need to increase to really support someone's health. Link Workers need to share the art of their community connector craft with each other, rather than reinforcing professionalisation.

However, I'm cynical about the road that social prescribing has travelled, and whether any of this can be reversed. The likely future, therefore, is a further institutionalisation of the profession. We already see the beginnings of professional organisation, academies, regulation and accountability structures. Link Workers & Health & Wellbeing Coaches are likely to become just another health profession, only expanding the reach of the NHS beyond medical problems into every corner of our lives, reinforcing healthism and turning us all into bio-citizens, leaving a path of community destruction in its wake. Future efforts for true "With" partnership between community connectors and institutions are likely to be displaced because "we already do that" and future community connectors are also likely to be heavily recruited into these professional ranks, both of which will severely hamper communities' healing process. From the perspective of communities and citizens, a future with social prescribing in it - without substantially changing its form urgently - is bleak. The time of future Gappers is likely to be consumed by holding back the Social Prescribing flood.

Chapter 13:
Online Bumping Spaces

Given the shift that has happened in my lifetime towards online space and the regular casting of the online world as an evil scourge on our communities and societies in the community-building world, I feel its important to provide an alternative perspective from someone in the generation that led the charge onto the online world and social media in particular

Many deride social media, often in the same breath as TV, for being the primary driver of the destruction of community (usually as they're blind to the larger agents of destruction). It might be fair for some of this to be levelled at TV, but in my own generation, I'm aware that TV has become much less of a staple in favour of social media and video games (many of them with multiplayer elements). This short chapter will mainly consider social media.

Social Media is neither wholly good nor wholly bad, but this is not a new statement. Others better than me have argued how social media can amplify the offline world - indeed, a huge number of my very real on-land friends and connections began online - and so I don't want to go over this. What I want to challenge is the rather accepted narrative that we should all be disciplined and cautious, ensuring that we don't succumb to the temptations of too much social media, leaving on-land community life to wither. It's probably clear by now that I don't like narratives like this.

How does the online world fit into our model? Earlier, we spoke about bumping spaces & fixing spaces. Bumping spaces are spaces that provide the conditions for natural, adult-to-adult connection to occur. Fixing spaces are deformed bumping spaces where people come to get fixed. Facebook, Twitter, Instagram and other social media are gigantic bumping spaces that encompass the whole globe, composed of huge numbers of small bumping subsystems (especially with Facebook). This provides a limitless opportunity to "bump" and create connections online. Nobody has yet figured out how to turn these into fixing spaces, which has protected them thus far.

Contrast this space with the on-land community, where architecturally, culturally, physically, financially and socially, bumping spaces everywhere are under attack. For example, we previously discussed how spaces like orchards, workshops and other institutions have been turned by funders into spaces where people go to get fixed, not places to be enjoyed organically.

But when we look at the specific experience of the generation in which I grew up, the one that led the charge into social media and the online world, we find more reasons for our abandonment of the on-land community.

Stories from the play of generations that preceded mine always sounded idyllic. Free roam of their surroundings, free from interference from parents, the police and their community. How that environment has been destroyed - indirectly through the loss of trust in community during our parent's generation - is the story of our generation, and the explanation of why we jumped into the online space headfirst - for our own sanity and survival.

My generation was denied access to the playgrounds and bumping spaces that we might normally have congregated in. Public spaces, like parks or swimming pools amongst others, were privatised, and we didn't have the pocket money to buy entry. Associations where we might have contributed our energy had been turned into structured, artificial places with red tape and hurdles that aren't very fun to negotiate. Property laws were enforced more strictly, denying us access to large swathes of land. Later, austerity closed further the few dedicated spaces we might turn to like youth centres. Finally, the cultural narrative around "chavs" and "ASBOs" denied us access to the few remaining spaces. My friends and I were kicked out of countless parks, libraries, skateparks and community centres for nothing more than looking like teenagers. My memories of interaction with my local community while growing up was one of suspicion and assumption that we were all out to steal handbags and stab people.

This isn't the fault of those residents, however. A side effect of the destruction of communities is a reduced perception of trust and safety, and in the 2000s, UK media and politicians hyped and exploited this fear for their own gain.

So, having been forced out of all spaces, we had nowhere left to go except roam the streets endlessly. We used to drift from street to street, park to park, with police chasing us around, informed by the calls of concerned residents, making sure we weren't up to no good. When we got cars, we switched from walking to driving from car park to car park, being pulled over by the police instead.

Having been forced into the last public spaces - the streets - we were now too public, intimidating and "anti-social". My village was even placed under a strict curfew by the local council and police force during my childhood for nothing more than children congregating at the village's crossroads.

It was these very reactions to the "chav" bogeyman that actually drove real anti-social behaviour and crime. With nothing else to do, we graffitied, trespassed, and broke things. We found abandoned buildings, woods or dunes where we could hide and do drugs & drink alcohol. I saw many lives ruined by this upbringing surrounded by exclusion, mistrust and injustice as well as by the reactions it drove in us. I'm sure that this experience was likely replicated across the UK and perhaps elsewhere. I know this environment has changed little for the new generation, except now as an adult, I see the very same process occurring from the opposite end.

When we contrast this environment with the limitless, freeing environment of social media, it is little wonder why, craving social contact, our generation immersed ourselves in the limitless social contact of social media.

And our environment has changed little as adults. Our communities are still bare of bumping spaces and contact. Where else can people go to find community?

Yes, social media has side effects, especially when used too much. Yes, social media is probably inferior to face to face contact (I think most people would prefer more face to face if we could!). But to enforce "discipline", limits and restriction onto people whose only way of connecting with others is via the internet is not only counterproductive but possibly lethal.

The solution is not to limit people's coping mechanisms for one of our greatest (and most unmet) needs just because some outsiders deem it unhealthy. The solution is to rebuild bumping spaces & community connections so that people have a choice, a way to find balance.

To bring people, especially children, out into the community and away from social media, they don't need discipline, and they certainly don't need more lectures, they need bumping spaces.

Conclusion

When we show up wanting to help someone or help ourselves, the cultural methods available to us are few. Throughout this book, I've attempted to show that there are more options available to us than we think and bring to conscious attention and celebrate some things we do naturally and unconsciously in our lives as valid ways of helping. I've also tried to show how the current state of "helping" is not down to malicious or lazy professionals or morally misguided or feckless citizens, but a result of the way that we choose to help.

To professionals working at the coalface, I hope this book has shown you why your personal gifts aren't being valued in the system, why your workload only grows bigger the more you help, and that those you're trying to help are not your enemy. I hope together we can release professionals from between the rock & the hard place of helping in a system that forces you to take tough decisions between what is allowed, what is right for the person you want to help and what will ultimately keep you and your family from starvation and homelessness. I hope I've illuminated a path where you can really help and care in the way you've always wanted. Remember, you can also be both a citizen in your own neighbourhood doing "By" as well as a professional doing "With" (or at least, as much "With" as you're allowed to do).

To institutional managers, I hope I've shown why things might not be going to plan. I hope the path I've shown is how we can rewild communities to naturally and organically take back some of the many plates you're being asked to juggle. This path involves courage to allow your employees to really care and to walk the "with" path alongside citizens.

And finally, to citizens, I hope I've shown that there is another way than constantly asking for permission and resources from outsiders. Many times, I've seen the extraordinary power that comes from neighbours escaping this paradigm and working together towards a better future, using the abundance of wealth they already have in their communities, but invisible until they go looking and connections are made.

Printed in Great Britain
by Amazon